MY HOUSE

A PLACE OF PRAYER
THE ORIGIN OF RIVALRY IN THE CHURCH

CHIOMA AFOKE

authorHOUSE

AuthorHouse™
1663 Liberty Drive
Bloomington, IN 47403
www.authorhouse.com
Phone: 833-262-8899

Published by AuthorHouse 11/21/2024

ISBN: 979-8-8230-3199-8 (sc)
ISBN: 979-8-8230-3200-1 (hc)
ISBN: 979-8-8230-3198-1 (e)

Library of Congress Control Number: 2024919376

Print information available on the last page.

This book is printed on acid-free paper.

Contents

Contents

Chapter One

My Altar
A Place of Power

An altar, in the context of the Christian faith, is a sacred space where believers can connect with God. It is a place of prayer and power, a place where God chooses to meet with you. It is also a place of covenant, as seen in the story of Abram. When Abram was concerned and wanted proof that God would give him everything he had promised, God told him to prepare a sacrifice. That sacrifice, and the location where it was offered, became an altar where God cemented the promises he made to Abram, and it became a covenant. Whenever you talk about a covenant, you talk about an altar; there is no covenant without an existing altar.

In the time of Moses, God told him where to meet with him and how to prepare for this meeting, which became a profound spiritual encounter for Moses. In this context, an encounter refers to a direct and personal experience of God's presence and communication. There is no encounter without the existence of an altar.

Every encounter you have ever had or will ever have, is a divine initiation. It is God who chooses when and where to meet with you. Even your hunger or desire to meet with God is a result of his prompting in your heart. When a quest or search is inspired in your heart, it is a way of God seeking or searching you out, Revelation 3:20. This should reassure you of his constant presence and his perfect timing in your life.

The most wonderful thing about God is his ability to communicate with his creation without a word. Whenever God thinks about you, it shows up as an encounter for you. These encounters can take various forms, such as a sudden feeling of peace in a difficult situation, a clear understanding of a complex issue, or a sense of direction when deciding. Just like when you think about something or someone, and suddenly you see that person, or the person calls you.

There is a superior force to the Mind of God, a force that makes him God. He said in Isaiah 14:24, "…Surely as I have thought, so shall it come to pass." This is not a mere statement, but a profound truth. It reveals that God has a mind, a mind that can think and shape reality. But the wonder of God's mind is this: whenever he thinks about you, the whole creation around you and your entire being will respond to his thoughts toward you. This should fill you with awe and wonder at the depth of God's thoughts and their impact on your life. As I said earlier, the mind has a very strong force, and those who understand how it works use it to benefit mankind.

In the book of John 6:44, Jesus made a weighty statement, "No one can come to me unless the Father who sent me draws him…" This is an overwhelming statement because often when you have a hunger or think about God, the moment your heart gravitates towards God, it is a sign that God is also thinking about you. We usually don't know that God put hunger in our hearts to seek after him. It is a part of the natural phenomenon of the mind, your ability to birth something through a thought process. God's love for humanity and His passion for man is that force of love that pulls us towards him.

When you begin to feel that pull to seek him, the love he has for you causes that pull.

David said in Psalm 27:8, "When thou said, seek ye my face; my heart said unto thee, thy face, LORD will I seek." When David made this statement, he responded to the prompting of God's invitation to know him. That hunger in David's heart was an understanding from David that God was calling him to seek his face. It is a very spiritual and also a physical attribute to train yourself to hearing the thoughts of God, because God can say many things without an echo of a voice, meaning God can make a billion statement without speaking out. This journey of seeking God's face is transformative, offering hope and inspiration.

This is to reiterate the statement that God is the one that influences your heart to begin to seek his face, that part of you that God made strictly for his occupant, that vacuum where the creator sits in your heart, triggers your quest for more of him. The quest to know and experience him more represents his love; a love that is all-encompassing, offering security and comfort. This love draws you to him.

From the beginning to the end of the Bible, it is God who consistently initiates encounters with man. In the book of Genesis, God not only created man but also planted a garden in the east of Eden, specifically designed as a meeting place between Him and the man He created. The Bible states that God would come down to the Garden in the cool of the day to commune with Adam. This act of God walking in the Garden in the cool of the day was for communication, a communion with Adam. The Garden, which God planted in Eden, was an altar where God met with Adam in the cool of the day. This raises the question, can any place where you meet with God be considered an altar? Let's delve deeper.

Abraham's encounters with God provide a personal perspective on altars. When he arrived in the land of Canaan, he built an altar there. After separating from his nephew Lot, the Lord visited him again, and Abraham built another altar. Abraham is known for building many altars, but the critical point is this: whenever God wanted to send a man on a journey in the Old Testament, he would show up, and wherever he showed up became a portal, a channel for people to access him. That is the reason why Abraham built many altars. As one with a history of idolatry, he understood an altar is a place of encounter, a place of access; hence, he built an altar each time he encountered God until God made a covenant with him.

Consider Jesus, who, though it was not called an altar, had significant encounters on the Mount of Transfiguration (Matthew 17:1-9). It was an encounter on a mount to the disciples, but to Jesus, it was his place of power, prayer, an altar. There were a few places where Jesus had altars of prayer, including the Mount of Transfiguration and the Garden of Gethsemane. The Garden of Gethsemane was a place where Jesus had direct access to heaven, much like the Garden in Eden, where God would come in the cool of the day to walk with Adam. Jesus experienced what Adam experienced in Eden at Gethsemane. You may recall when Jesus said to the scribes and the Pharisees,' Whatever I see my Father do, that's what I do' (John 5:19b). Jesus had access and a physical communion with the Father, witnessing the Father perform those miracles before He performed them (John 5:18-20).

What I am saying, in essence, is this: Jesus experienced the Father physically, the same way Adam did in the Garden of Eden. That is why it was recounted that Jesus sweated blood at the tail end of his ministry, at the Garden of Gethsemane (Luke 22:44), because he experienced the withdrawal of God's physical presence from him. When the sin of Adam was placed on Jesus, it had to be in the Garden, and God withdrew his physical presence from Jesus, the same way he withdrew from Adam at the Garden of Eden. In other words, Gethsemane was a replica of the Garden of Eden.

The point that I am trying to make is this, an altar is a place of power, a place of prayer, a place of sacrifice, and a place of meeting between God and man. The level of power that proceeds out of your altar can be linked to the level of activities on your altar. When I say activities, I mean communication which could be in form of prayer, worship, meditations etc. between God and man. The level of activities from your altar generates the power to your altar. In other words, the fewer activities you have on your altar, the less power you have to it. Above all, there is no altar without a sacrifice.

For example, in the Garden called Eden, the Bible said it had a river that flowed into four channels (Genesis 2:8-10). These channels represented the activities that were going on in Eden. Rivers flow from altars, and they are known as the rivers of living water (John 7:38). These 'Rivers of living water' symbolize the spiritual nourishment and life that flow from our altars, sustaining our relationship with God.

What I am saying from the beginning is this, an altar is a place of prayer and encounter, and only God determines how and when you encounter him; if he ever shows up in your home, build him an altar, and make sure you allow activities to be a daily thing. If he showed up in your home, it is because he wants a relationship with you, he wants something deeper with you, and you must cultivate that ground. This is a personal invitation from God to you, a sign of his desire for a unique and special relationship with you.

Whenever God shows up, you will surely know, because you will notice some changes, and some spiritual manifestations that will alert you that God is physically around. These manifestations can include a sense of peace, a deep conviction, or a heightened awareness of His presence, depending on your level of sensitivity. If you notice that God is calling you to a deeper relationship, make out time, build him an altar (meeting place) where you could easily connect with him.

Finally, even though God is the one to determine the part of him you encounter or experience, you do have a part or parts to play. Just as I said, when you notice or sense that God is visiting you, the way you respond to his presence has a lot to do with how he proceeds with you. If your response is that of no interest, he will withdraw, but will continue to pursue after you until you start beckoning on him. A positive response could be engaging in prayer, reading scripture, or reflecting on His teachings.

When I say to build an altar of prayer here, it does not necessarily mean a physical altar; you may designate a place to speak to God privately without distractions. It is the example Jesus taught us: he would move away from his disciples and the multitude of people thronging him to a place of prayer. For Jesus, he used mountains and deserts to prepare for his ministry (Mark 1:12-13). Where is your waiting place? It could be a designated room in your home or a different location. Wait in Zion, a spiritual place, until you encounter power and receive the capacity for your assignment.

Above all, you are the most desirable altar God seeks to dwell in, you can encounter God daily within you. Prepare yourself, a living sacrifice unto him, that is his desire for you, and it is your own reasonable service, Romans 12:1. This is a testament to God's love for you, his desire to be close to you, and his cherishing of your spiritual journey.

Chapter Two

Jesus of Nazareth
Who is He?

Jesus was baptized by John the Baptist at River Jordan, and as soon as he stepped out of the river, the heavens opened, and God the Father Spoke, Mark1:10-11. Have you ever asked who God spoke to and why? We will discuss that statement in detail next.

Looking at the baptism of Jesus as recorded by Matthew

The Bible said in the book of Mathew 3:11-12 that John the Baptist announced the coming of the Messiah, who will baptize the people with the Holy Ghost and fire. While he was still speaking, Jesus appeared from Galilei to be baptized. It is very worthy to note here that John the Baptist was the cousin of Jesus of Nazareth, and they grew up together.

In other words, John and Jesus could have been friends growing up and did things together as cousins. They could have played soccer or basketball together, perhaps fetched water and firewood together. Oh yes! Jesus was also someone's biological son; Mary was her name. As a natural son of Mary, do you think Jesus did not do some housework, some chores? Did he help his father do some carpentry work? That's why the people were offended at him when he started talking Godly, in the sense of being the Son of God, because they knew his mother and his father, the carpenter.

"Coming to His hometown, He taught the people in their synagogue, and they were astonished. Where did this man get such wisdom and miraculous powers they asked? Isn't this the carpenter's son? Isn't His mother's name Mary, and aren't His brothers James, Joseph, Simon, and Judas?" (Mathew 13:55-56)

This is to provoke your thoughts on where I am going and what will be discussed here in this chapter. Part of the issues John the Baptist had with Jesus after he knew that he was the Messiah was due to their close relationship and shared experiences. They ate together, did things together, possibly bathed together as little boys. Remember that John the Baptist was only six months older than Jesus of Nazareth? In Luke 1:36, the angel Gabriel who brought about the news of the conception and the birth of Jesus to his mother trying to convince her about the possibility of bearing a baby without the natural help of a man, but by the Holy Ghost, told Mary that Elizabeth her cousin who was past menopaused was already pregnant for six months with John the Baptist.

This news lightened Mary up, and the Bible says she packed her things and ran out in excitement to visit Elizabeth. And when Elizabeth saw her, the baby in her womb (John the Baptist) leaped for Joy, (Luke 1:39-42). What was the possibility that John would have failed Jesus earlier if he had knowledge of him being the Messiah? John asked God few times who the Messiah was, but the response he got was that whomever the Spirit descended on and remained with, is the Messiah. It also means that John was in anticipation to meet the Messiah, until he realized it was Jesus his cousin brother. It also means that Mary contained the information given to her by the angel who visited her securely and protected Jesus well from envious harm from family members.

John and Jesus, being cousins, spent a significant amount of time together. John, with a deep sense of purpose, continually sought God's guidance on the identity of the Messiah. His eagerness to fulfill his role as the forerunner of the Messiah was palpable, as he earnestly desired to know who the Messiah would be.

One momentous day, God revealed to John the divine sign that would identify the Messiah. He was told that the man on whom the Spirit would descend and remain was the chosen one, the one who would baptize with the Holy Spirit. John, in awe of this revelation, declared, "I myself did not know Him, but the One who sent me to baptize with water told me, 'The man on whom you see the Spirit descend and rest, is He who will baptize with the Holy Spirit." (John 1:33).

It means that the Holy Ghost can descend and lift off people as well. This was still the period of the Old Testament, and the Holy Ghost was popularly known for descending on people, leading them, then lifts off from them. Many examples are written in Ezekiel 3:22 and 37:1. The hand of the LORD there represents the Holy Spirit.

As I was saying, John didn't know that Jesus was the Messiah, until during his baptism. And as soon as he declared that one was coming who would baptize the people with Holy Spirit and fire, Jesus showed up (Mathew 3:13).

As soon as Jesus was baptized, a dramatic and awe-inspiring moment unfolded. The heavens opened, and the Spirit descended on him like a dove. Then, a voice from heaven proclaimed, "This is my beloved Son, in whom I am well pleased" (Mathew 3:17). The significance and power of this event were undeniable.

Who was this voice Confirming to?

As you immerse yourself in Mark 1:11's accounts, a profound revelation unfolds: "And a voice came from heaven: 'You are My beloved Son; in You I am well pleased.' This divine confirmation of Jesus as the beloved Son of God resonates with awe-inspiring reverence.

Also, as recorded by Luke 3:22, the account reads, "And the Holy Spirit descended on him in a bodily form like a dove. And a voice came from heaven: "You are My beloved Son; in You, I am well pleased."

I truly believe that God the Father was speaking directly to Jesus to confirm that he is already pleased with him as a son. This is very important to note because when you get to Jesus's temptations, you will realize why God the Father had to confirm to Jesus of Nazareth that he is indeed the true son of God.

The Bible said that Jesus was led by the Holy Ghost to be tempted by the Devil (Mathew 4:1). This statement alone is packed with many mysteries; how could the Holy Spirit lead Jesus to a place where he would be tempted? Child of God, embrace yourself very well because temptations and trials are part of what we go through to be confirmed; if you have not been tempted, you have not been confirmed. God does not tempt you, as indicated in the book of James 1:13: "...God cannot be tempted by evil and cannot temp you." But God could allow you to be tempted; Job is a perfect example. To God, it is a trial of your faith; to the Devil, he wants to lure you into sin.

In other words, to be confirmed as a true child of God, you must go through trials and temptations. No one is born a champion; you acquire your championship by fighting battles and wars.

Therefore, it was so important for Jesus to tell us that we are more than conquerors (Romans 8:37), not because he fought all the battles but because he had already won the major battles, which included defeating the powers behind the battle, the Devil. So, any other battle we fight is to prove our championship.

Jesus has already secured the victory for us; we fight to establish it. You have been made a victor. This truth should bolster your confidence in him (Christ). If he has already won, then you should stand your ground; that's how you establish your victory. This assurance of victory should fill you with confidence and strength as you face your battles.

Satan challenges Jesus Identity

Do you remember I told you earlier that it was important that God the Father affirm Jesus's true identity? He (Jesus) would need that statement and the reinforcement of that knowledge.

Later in the next chapter, you will see through the wilderness, which the Holy Spirit led Jesus into. This divine guidance was crucial for Jesus's confirmation as the Beloved Son of God, a reassurance he would need upon exiting the wilderness. Jesus's confirmation was vital because it empowered him to cast out devils and perform other miraculous deeds. The next chapter will discuss in detail on how Satan attacked Jesus' identity.

Let me bring you to the wilderness where the devil tempted Jesus; inside this wilderness were all kinds of wild beasts, serpents, and scorpions. They contended with him while in the wilderness; the serpent and the scorpion hauled at him. I learned this from the Holy Spirit. The reason why Jesus told you to tread on the serpent and scorpion in Luke 10:19 was because while in the wilderness, he did the same. Jesus would never ask you to do something he had not already done. His doing it is to prove to you that you can also do the same; he was a hundred percent man and a hundred percent God.

What I am saying is that in the wilderness, serpents and scorpions came at him, just the same way the serpent bit Paul, the apostle in Act 28:3; Jesus got a taste of the serpent's bite. What do you think he did with them? He crushed them like a winepress. When you check the word "Tread," as used in Luke 10:19, it is the same word used in Revelation 14:20, which describes the wrath of God against his enemies.

In other words, Jesus of Nazareth, while in the wilderness, was bitten by the serpent and the scorpion, and he treaded upon them with his foot. I know you are feeling slightly jittery about what I just said. Let me take you to the book of Mark 1:13: "And He was there in the wilderness forty days, tempted by Satan, and was with the wild beasts; and the angels ministered to him."

The first thing to ask here is, why did the Bible have to mention that he was with wild beasts? The answer is what I just told you: the wild beasts included the serpent and the scorpion that bit him. Secondly, why did the Bible mention that the Angels ministered to him? How do you read the scripture? Do you ask the Holy Spirit questions about what you don't understand in the scripture? Because that's how to read the scripture properly.

When Jesus was attacked by Satan using the wild beasts, the angels ministered to him. What else were angels doing for him? I believe this truth because I have experienced it.

Jesus of Nazareth was fasting and praying in the wilderness to prepare him for his ministry, and he was being attacked in the wilderness by Satan using wild beasts. Jesus was not only tempted in the wilderness, but he was also attacked seriously by Satan and his demons. It was because of some of these attacks that led to him at one point questioning his true identity. He was tempted to think, "If you are the son of God...how could these things happen to you?".

Chapter Three

The Origin of Rivalry in the Church
Understanding Your Assignment

Jesus prayed the most essential prayer ever prayed by any man in the book of John 17. He started off by acknowledging God the Father as the one who has supremacy of all flesh, and the power to glorify anyone in heaven and earth.

In John 17:2, Jesus said, "As thou have given him power over all flesh, that he should give eternal life to as many as thou hast given him." Here, two major principles were elicited: God the Father gives you the power to reach people. We learn through the prayer of Jesus of Nazareth that it is God who gives you authority over a specific population and a particular people. He gives you the power to subdue before anything else. Jesus is saying here that you do not have the power to cover a specific population or location if it's not given to you from above. This divine empowerment is a transformation. It's the power to bring eternal life to as many as God has given you. This divine empowerment is the key to your ministry; it inspires and motivates you to reach your full potential.

This is precisely why Jesus instructed his disciples to remain in Jerusalem until they were given power from above, as stated in Luke 24:49. Many fail or become disheartened in their ministry because they have not adhered to this aspect of Jesus' command. If Jesus required his disciples to wait until they were empowered from on High, would he expect any less from you? Would he advise you to move forward prematurely? He said, 'Stay in Jerusalem until you receive power.' So, why are you not staying?

Jerusalem, in this context, also represents the heavenly realms, where power can be assessed (Hebrew 12:22). As I said in Chapter One of this book, when you notice that God is stirring your heart to something, the first thing to do is to build an altar of prayer. Remember, waiting for power from above is not a delay; it's a divine guidance that will direct your steps in your ministry.

God must give you power before an assignment; it's not the reverse. Some people run off to a perceived assignment without a release of power to them. If you believe that God is calling you to something, don't take off without power; it leads to frustrations in ministry. Many are falling asleep, and by the waysides because they skipped this process of tarrying in Jerusalem until the power comes. The Greek word (Tarry)here is "Kathizo," which means to sit down or stay in a place. Please take a seat, which means it's probably not a one-day or a few hours thing. It may take days, months, and sometimes years until you are in the place of power. Please wait; this is the only way to be unique in your assignment. Wait until you receive power from the father. Remember, patience is a virtue, and you will find peace and reassurance in this waiting. Don't forget that waiting is not an idling, while you are waiting you may be going through a spiritual process and encounters, learn to wait efficiently.

The second thing we learn from this verse is that God the Father brings the people you will reach. Jesus by the Spirit said it this way, "that he should give eternal life to those you have given to him, John 17:2b. There is a gravitational force in you, according to the power that works in you, and that power that works in you is based on the knowledge you have of God, who gave you the power. When God gives you power, there are specific locations and certain people for whom power is meant to work.

As I said earlier, Jesus told his disciples to remain in Jerusalem for this exact reason, and he (Jesus) also remained in Jerusalem until he officially died. Jesus was originally sent to the lost sheep of Israel and could not manifest in the full capacity of his ministry until he was led into the wilderness, a place of waiting, an altar where he encountered God, angels, and even Satan. That means that even in the place of your waiting, the devils can challenge you and question your identity, but do not be discouraged; you will walk in power when your waiting is completed.

That's why Jesus instructed his disciples to pray in the upper room until they received power from on high. There is a level of power that only God can give to you; no man can give you that power. Even if you rent that power as did the disciples of Jesus before his death, you will still have limitations. The disciples, at a point, couldn't cast out a demon from a Lunatic boy; they tried but failed until they had to consult the one who gave them the power, the source of the power. That foul spirit of deaf and dumb was cast out of the little boy by Jesus in few minutes. Mathew 17:14-18.

Certain demons you cannot cast out if you are not the true possessor of the powers of God. When God the Father gave Jesus' power over all flesh, as stated in John 17:2, he also gave him the people to manifest that power to; there are certain population that your God given power is set for, but don't forget that faith can change things.

That's why Jesus said to a woman who was foreign to Israel when she came to ask for healing for her daughter, "You do not give the children's bread to dogs." Mathew 16:22-28. But before this statement, he said to the woman," I am not sent but to the lost sheep of the house of Israel. This means that the power he received to heal is only for the lost sheep of the house of Israel, but the woman could draw out of Jesus with her wisdom and perseverance.

As I was saying, it is God that gives you power, and it is also God that will map out a location for you to reach. If you don't have that power yet, don't try reaching out to people. There is a specific magnetic field that you cover by the power of God in you, and when you continue to wait on God, He can choose to increase your territory by the measure of the power he has released into you. If you know this, you will not fight other men of God or those who manifest the power of God; you will not desire to be like someone else because every child of God is uniquely made and can manifest uniquely according to the power that lies in them.

He said to Joshua, "Wherever the sole of your foot will tread upon, I have given to you," and also assured him about extending his territory, Joshua 1:3-5. It is God who meticulously maps out your territory and the sphere you are to cover, based on your assignment, a territory can be subdued under you. And the people that are assigned unto you, God will give you power over them, not to intimidate them, but to give them eternal life, John 17:2b. You are not alone in this journey, for God is always there, guiding and supporting you in your mission.

It also means, when people follow you or are attracted to you, it is because they are hungry for the eternal life that you carry. This 'eternal life' is not just about living forever, but it's a quality of life that comes from a deep personal relationship with God. And if you don't give them that which you purposed to give them, they will disperse.

At some point, John the Baptist began to question Jesus because the people moved away from him and began to seek after Jesus, including his disciples. At this point, he questioned if Jesus was the Messiah. We will discuss this in detail next.

When you lose focus on your assignment and the territory God assigned to you, the people will seek pasture from another, a common reaction of man; they will migrate to another source of life.

In other words, there are specific populations you are supposed to reach according to your assigned purpose on earth, and certain people will not stay in your circle of influence, no matter what you do. Do you know why? Because you have nothing for them. Sitting under you will only make them degenerate and cause problems. As a minister of the gospel of Jesus Christ, you are not meant to reach everyone; if you force it, they will cause you harm. Respect their autonomy and understand that they have the power to choose their spiritual path.

Stay in God until you are endowed with power; then, you will also receive an audience from God, John 17:2. The audience or the population that will be magnetic to you are those you have been empowered to reach. Don't fight over members; they are God's people, not yours.

Another significant lesson from Jesus's prayer is in his statement in John 17:6, "I have manifested thine name...thine they were, and you gave them to me." This is a powerful reminder. The people you have are the people of God. They are God's children whom he entrusted to you as a shepherd to guide and protect. You are accountable for them because God has given them to you. This responsibility underscores the value and importance of your role as a minister.

If you ever understand how delicate it is that God took his children and handed them to you to watch over them, you will never treat people like you own them. You don't own anyone, not the people of the world, and not the Church people; they don't belong to you, they belong to the Father, the God of all flesh (Jeremiah 32:27). Once you know this, you will treat people respectfully. And you will be more responsible and accountable, knowing that God is watching over you and the people he gave you to manage.

Another crucial lesson we learn here is from Jesus's words, "I have manifested thy name unto the men which thou gavest me out of the world: thine they were, and thou gavest them me; and they have kept thy word." (John 17:6 KJV). "I spelled out your character in detail. To the men and women, you gave me. They were yours in the first place; Then you gave them to me." (John 17:6 MSG).

This statement underscores a fundamental principle: as a minister, you are to manifest the name of God to the people, not your own name; the name of Jesus possesses his character, and personality. If Jesus is your example, as you claim, then you must follow his lead and manifest his name on earth, his name is above every other name (Jesus Christ of Nazareth). This principle should inspire and guide your actions as a minister.

Remember what Jesus was doing here? He was praying for himself and his disciples. First, Jesus asked the Father to glorify him (Jesus the Son). The Father should glorify him because he manifested the Father's name and glorified the Father by finishing his assignment correctly. This brings us to the fourth thing we learn from Jesus's prayer.

"I have glorified thee on the earth: I have finished the work which thou gavest me to do. And now, O Father, glorify thou me with thine own self with the glory which I had with thee before the world was" (John 17:4-5).

As you delve deeper into John 17:4, you will come to understand that God has specifically chosen and assigned you to work on this earth. Your assignment is not a random task but a divine calling, a unique and special task tailored for you by God. This is how you discern that you are in line with God's purpose for your life and that you are fulfilling your destiny. Your assignment is intricately linked to the population you were sent to meet or serve.

Let me digress a little to Philippians 2:5-7, "Let this mind be in you which was also in Christ Jesus, who, being in the form of God, did not consider it robbery to be equal with God, but made Himself of no reputation, taking the form of a bondservant, *and* coming in the likeness of men." Here, Paul admonishes the believers of Jesus Christ to have the same mindset that Jesus had while on earth. According to Paul, even though Jesus knew he was equal to God, he took on another form as a servant. Meaning that Jesus, as God in the flesh, came to humanity, his creation, to serve them and not the other way around. In line with what we are discussing here, Jesus prayed to the Father that he had finished the work (assignment) he had been assigned to do. That was his service to humanity, a specific population.

Remember, it is you who must take up the form of a servant. God doesn't make you a servant; you choose to humble yourself and become one. When you embrace this form of servant, Grace is released unto you for service. This act of humility is not a sign of weakness but a powerful tool in your service to God and humanity. It empowers you to serve with Grace and strength, making you capable of fulfilling your divine calling.

Remember, your assignment comes after you have been assigned a population to reach. To fulfill this assignment, you must take on the form of a servant. When you embrace this form of a servant, the grace of humility will be released upon you, leading to your glorification. God does not glorify people who are outside their assignment. Therefore, pray fervently for your eyes to be opened to the population you are to serve, and the assignment given to you. With God's unwavering guidance, you will experience your glory, feeling reassured and connected to him.

In John 17:4, Jesus says that he fulfilled his purpose on earth; by the time he prayed this prayer, he had not died on the cross, but he prayed it out of faith, knowing that the future had already been established.

The fifth thing we learn from Jesus's prayer is in John 17:5, "O Father, glorify thou me with thine own self with the glory which I had with thee before the world was" (John 17:5).

Jesus is saying there is a certain glory he had with the Father before he stepped down from that glory to serve humanity. This 'glory' refers to the divine essence and power that Jesus possessed as the Son of God. Likewise, every child of God here on earth had a certain glory in God; you enjoyed a certain level of divine favor and power, or, better said, you had a certain level of divine glory in God as a spirit before you became flesh. That glory was only given to you by God the Father, and it's that divine favor and power that Jesus prayed to the Father to restore to him.

Many children of God find it a struggle to attain the glory on earth. This is a clear indication that you must follow the process of actualizing God's purpose and your assigned destiny. This process involves seeking God's will for your life, aligning your actions with his teachings, and persevering in faith despite challenges. By doing so, you will be able to attain the level of glory that God has destined for you on earth.

That's what Paul said when he wrote to his son Timothy, "I have fought the good fight, I have finished the race, I have kept the faith. Now there is in store for me the crown of righteousness, which the

Lord, the righteous Judge, will award to me on that day and not only to me but also to all who have longed for his appearing." 2 Timothy 4:7-8.

Before the world began, you existed in God the Father as a spirit, and your spirit remembers your glory with the Father. The key to accessing this glory is fulfilling your destined purpose on earth. When you do, your spirit is at peace, and you feel a sense of completeness. This reassurance and contentment are what that glory brings to you, filling you with a profound sense of fulfillment.

The sixth thing Jesus addressed in his prayer is in John 17:7-8, "For the message you gave me, I gave them; And they took it, and were convinced that I came from you. They believed that you sent me" (MSG).

As a minister of the Gospel of Jesus Christ, your primary responsibility is to evaluate the people you serve, or the people God has entrusted to you. According to the words of Jesus of Nazareth in this chapter, you evaluate the people under your covering by the message you have preached to them. This message about God is not to be taken lightly, as it holds the key to their spiritual growth and understanding.

What do they know about God? Many ministers of the Gospel have successfully taught the people about themselves; many of the people of God, know just a tiny bit of God, but everything about their pastor or their minister. As a man of God, your success, is in the level of the knowledge of God that you have passed unto the people that you cover. It's not enough to just impart this knowledge; the people should be able to believe this message and be convinced that you proceeded from God. Their belief and conviction are crucial for their spiritual journey.

In other words, did you impact this population with knowledge about yourself or God? The people can know everything about you but nothing about God. This is what Jesus was addressing here; he said the people have known that everything I have is from you, meaning you are not your own either. You didn't manifest these powers out of nowhere; they were given to you by God, whose you are.

Jesus continued to elaborate on how he achieved success in ministry; the word he received from God was the same word he gave to the people and not his word. Don't forget that Jesus, who is also known as the word, was the one speaking to the Father, being specific on what he fed his people, the actual word from the Father.

This brings me to another point: after you have received your assignment from the Father, you are not to run ministry independently of the Father; you still stay connected to the Father because He is the one who gives you wisdom on how to handle the people you are assigned to reach. In other words, he teaches you what to feed the people to keep them connected to him. This connection is not just important, it is crucial. Feeding the flock, the proper meal (the word of God) is the secret to church growth, as it proves to the people that you have access to the Father.

In summary, Jesus, through his prayer, told us many things, such as how to begin and end a ministry on earth. You must start with the father and be patient until you receive power, pointing you to your assignment. Then, your assignment will point you to the population and your audience, and you can finish well by glorifying God. Placing the name of God above your name and the purpose of God above your purpose.

One final thought here is Jesus stated in his prayer saying, "I have manifested your name unto them "John 17:6. It's only the Name that can do many things, miracles, healing, casting out devils, etc. his disciples once said, "the devils are subjects unto us, in your name," Luke 10:17. You should then know that your name will not work for the people of God because the devils are not subjected to your name but the name of Jesus Christ of Nazareth.

The Rivalry of John the Baptist
Jesus of Nazareth! Are You the Messiah?

Jesus said, "A man's enemies shall be those of his own household" (Matthew 10:36). Illustrating the intensity of vision and purpose and the importance of staying focused on one's calling despite family rejection. Jesus had firsthand experience of the above statement; the Bible says his brothers did not believe in him, which could have been a significant challenge in his ministry (John 7:5). It could also have affected his mother to some extent, who was the one who carried the vision of birthing the son of the Holy Spirit, Luke 1:35.

For the majority of his ministry on earth, Jesus grappled with his family's disbelief. This struggle was why his mother and brothers came looking for him at one point to bring him home; they heard of what he was saying and doing and how he claimed to be God in the flesh.

They had already doubted and challenged him at home about the miracles he performed and his claims to be from above, a feeling of great embarrassment in his brothers. They came looking to speak to him because of the complaint they got from people that Jesus had become blasphemous in his statements. So, they came to talk to him and bring him home. That is why Jesus said, "Who is my mother, and who are my brethren? For whoever shall do the will of my father in heaven is my brother, sister, and mother" (Matthew 12:46-50).

Though, his brethren later believed in him after his resurrection and ascension into heaven.

John the Baptist was a man who had a divine mandate, a mission of utmost importance, to forerun for Jesus of Nazareth. In the scripture above (Matthew 10:36), Jesus made a very important point about the enemy within one's family, a part of the battle that one must contend with to get to destiny.

Jesus was indirectly speaking to his disciples about John the Baptist, who had started preaching a different gospel and had deviated from the gospel of the kingdom. At some point, we will delve into John the Baptist's mistakes and the cause of his death.

Jesus said to those whom John the Baptist sent to him, "Go back and tell John what you hear and see; the blind receive sight, the lame walk, the lepers are cleansed, the deaf hear, the dead are raised, and the good news is preached to the poor" (Mathew 11:4). Illustrating what gospel John was supposed to preach, Jesus made this statement after John started questioning his messiahship and his identity as the son of God.

When you look closer, you will see that Jesus had already perceived that John would go this route with him; that is why he had said many things to his disciples in the prior chapter. He was not direct in many of his statements about John in Matthew 10: 24-36, but after these statements, John sent his disciples to question Jesus' true identity. When you lose focus on God's vision, many things start happening to you, including questioning your true identity. Not only did John question Jesus's identity, but he also doubted his own identity. At some point, John was a bit confused about his true identity, a grave consequence of losing focus on his divine mandate.

Let me clarify, at one point, the multitude asked John about his identity. While he was explicit about his identity, as stated in Isaiah

40:3, he denied being in the spirit of Elijah, as proclaimed by the angel who visited his father, Zachariah, before his birth. This denial adds a layer of complexity to John's identity and made it more difficult for the multitudes who came to him to seek the Messiah.

John the Baptist's purpose on earth was not just singular, but of immense significance. His role was to prepare the ground for Jesus, to pave the way, and to level the ground so Jesus could carry out his ministry. His contribution was not just important, but crucial in the context of Jesus's mission. It underscored the weight of his role in Jesus's journey and the profound impact he had on the unfolding of the divine plan for humanity.

John, with his unique and singular destiny, was tasked with the crucial mission of preparing the people and the land for the gospel of the Kingdom. Had his work been fully accomplished, it would have significantly reduced the challenges Jesus faced. His purpose was to instill a sense of eager anticipation and readiness among the people for Jesus' imminent arrival.

In Luke 3:5, "Every valley shall be filled in, every mountain and hill made low. The crooked roads shall become straight, the rough ways smooth" which is the continuation of the prophesy in Isaiah 40:3-5. John was prophesied about; his purpose was to prepare the way of the Lord by making his part straight. The valleys should be filled with people, and the mountains and the hills leveled to accommodate people who would throng to hear Jesus speak because of the gospel that John the Baptist was to preach.

The effect of John's purpose was to make sure that all flesh saw the salvation of the Lord in the person of Jesus of Nazareth. Luke 3:6. "All flesh shall see." The word "shall see" here is the Greek word "Horan" which means to perceive. The purpose and the effect of John's ministry was that every flesh would at least perceive, discern, and experience the salvation of God, which was the Kingdom of God. That is the reason Jesus reiterated to John's disciples in Matthew 11:4, the right message of the Kingdom, which John was supposed to be part of, but rivalry took hold of him.

John the Baptist did not completely finish preaching the gospel he was supposed to preach. He started well with the right message but veered off somehow. John was anointed from his mother's womb with an unusual anointing for evangelism, a 'Mimshack anointing' that empowered him to cover territories with his message. This anointing made it possible for anyone who heard John speak to pay attention to him. Remember I said earlier that God is the one who appoints a population that you are to reach with the empowerment he gives to you. In other words, the people John was to reach for Jesus were already prepared, but did John reach them? Let's find out.

When the Angel who announced about John the Baptist visited his father, Zachariah, he said in Luke 1:15-16, "...he shall be filled with the Holy Ghost from his mother's womb, and he shall turn many of the children of Israel to God." John was supposed to reach above and exceed many Jewish territories in preparation for the gospel of Jesus Christ.

John's anointing was similar to that of Lucifer, an anointing that could turn territories into valleys and make the grounds plain. This comparison does not equate John with Lucifer but illustrates the power of John's anointing. Lucifer used his anointing to turn the earth into a voided place when he was cast out of heaven and made the light turn into darkness. This is just a side note to highlight the power of John's anointing.

John, while in prison, was offended at Jesus for a few things, one of them being that he did not visit him or rescue him from prison. You have to understand one thing about John, he grew up with Jesus, as a cousin, so there were things he knew about Jesus that many did not know, but these were not enough to prevent his feelings of offense.

The most important point here is, John got distracted, and he preached a different gospel. While Jesus was in the wilderness, John announced the arrival of the kingdom of God which was the person of Jesus. This was the gospel John was supposed to continue to preach, there by gathering the multitude in preparation to receive the gospel of the kingdom which Jesus was to preach after he returned from the wilderness.

As led by the spirit, John preached about repentance as recorded in Luke 3:3, and by his preaching, the valley would be filled with people, waiting to receive the salvation that Jesus was to offer them afterward. But when Jesus returned from the Wilderness, John was already derailing from the gospel he was supposed to preach.

John the Baptist did not lose focus because he did not understand his purpose, he understood his purpose very well. What caused John to lose focus was his Rivalry over the ministry of Jesus. The Bible said when John was told of the things Jesus was doing, how his fame was rapidly spreading, John sent his disciples to question Jesus of his identity, Matthew 11:2-3.

Jesus who in the wilderness being prepared by the Holy Ghost for the ministry, believed John was preparing the way for him. Truly, when John preached the gospel of the kingdom, his disciples began to abandon him for Jesus, which John saw as a problem, forgetting he was supposed to point people to Jesus, and make disciples for Jesus of Nazareth, not himself. When people began to leave John for Jesus, he became a bit competitive, and that's where his rivalry over

Jesus started. He began to raise disciples who he though different doctrines away from the doctrine of Jesus Christ.

The Bible says in John 1:35-37 that John stood with his disciples while still very excited about Jesus; he looked at Jesus as he walked by and said, "Behold, the Lamb of God!" And two of his disciples left him for Jesus, a very significant factor that made John look at Jesus differently; and also, a contributing factor to the reason why he preached a different gospel. John who was a center of attraction, became less popular than Jesus, and that was not fun.

Have you ever wondered what was going through John's mind to have his spotlight taken over by his cousin, whom he had not known was the True Messiah? If John had not lost focus and followed his purpose on earth, it would have been a joy to see Jesus glorified. Instead, John preached a different gospel, as Jesus became the center of attention.

John was in a tough place here; first, he was arrested and placed in a prison awaiting trial but felt dejected because not even his cousin, whom he was a forerunner to came to visit him. He was in a state of mental challenge, just like his prototype Elijah when he had finished the crusade where he slaughtered over four hundreds prophets of Baal at Mount Carmel. Jezebel threatened his life, he became suicidal (1 Kings 19:1-3), a problem characterized by mental instability. John was in the same situation, he had just been arrested for speaking against Herodians, representing the Jezebel of the Modern Day then.

Today, in the body of Christ, many fight over members they believe to be their disciples; men of God fight one another for this same reason. Many children of God suffer from this dysfunctional problem in ministry, it is the tantrum of ministers of the gospel. It happened in the days of the apostles of Jesus Christ and is still happening

29

today. Paul the apostle once addressed it where he reminded the believers of Jesus Christ about what the true focus should be. When you go through 1 Corinthians 1:10-12 and 1 Corinthians 3:1-10, Apostle Paul mentions the focus of this gospel; it should be all about Jesus Christ, who is the true foundation.

In essence, at a certain point, John the Baptist lost focus and instead of making disciples for Jesus Christ, he began to build his empire. This shift in focus had significant implications for his ministry and the spread of the gospel.

Whenever you see a minister of the gospel who has a questionable focus, one thing you will notice is in his character, he becomes very abusive. This abusive behavior is not just a personal flaw, it also has significant implications for his ministry and the people he is meant to reach.

Since John is our focus here, we will examine how his sudden change in character towards the people he was anointed to reach affected their reaction to Jesus and the gospel of salvation. At a point, John the Baptist became verbally abusive towards the population he was supposed to reach, he started cursing them, and was verbally intolerant towards them.

Don't forget I said earlier that God gives you a population to reach; the people who gathered to hear from John had already been predestined to harken unto his voice, including Herod the Agrippa. The Bible said that King Herod liked listening to him, which means he was also one of the people John was supposed to reach, but he preached the wrong gospel. The king Herod, listened to John even when his message was very unpleasant, but the reason he listened was because he was expecting the message of the kingdom. John needed to point him to Jesus; perhaps he would have received salvation.

In Luke 3:7, the multitudes gathered to hear John's preaching and to be baptized, but what they heard from him shocked them. John said to them, "You generation of vipers, who hath warned you to flee from the wrath to come?'

Let me ask you a question, when you get into a church, looking to hear from a man of God like John, and you are called names, wouldn't you be confused? John's population got confused; they came to receive the kingdom and get baptized in preparation to receive the Messiah but rather got verbally abused.

Many of them, bewildered and uncertain, asked in confusion, "What shall we do then"? (Luke 3:10).

John lost focus, so his message changed, which was part of what got him in trouble. When you read the book of Luke 3:11-14, John's response to their question was a repetition of the law of Moses. The people already knew what the law of Moses said, they moved around with copies of the law, they were hungry for the Messiah, to receive salvation. Instead, John continued to speak the laws of Moses to them.

The people eagerly and expectantly awaiting the Messiah, were left wondering after John repeated the laws of Moses to them. They asked if he was the Messiah? their hearts filled with hope and anticipation. (Luke 3:15 "...the people were in expectation, and all men mused in their hearts of John, whether he was the Christ or not"). Because they came in expectation to meet the Messiah.

John was anointed to reach the people whose hearts were hardened by the law of Moses; that's what the law does to peoples' hearts: harden them. In this case, the people were prepared by God to harken to John's voice, which was to soften their hearts towards receiving the Messiah, Jesus of Nazareth. Jesus encountered problems in reaching the people when he started his ministry. This was why Jesus had to reach out to his disciples since John moved on with his own agenda, his gospel, which ended his ministry.

This question comes to mind: if you are a forerunner of someone, a person who comes before and prepares the way for another, and the person appears on the scene, do you disappear or stay with the person you are forerunning for? This concept of a forerunner is crucial to understanding the relationship between John and Jesus and the impact of their actions on their ministries.

John was supposed to be Jesus' chief disciple, one of his inner circles, but he was not. His actions, driven by rivalry with Jesus, confused the people about his identity. If John was not in rivalry with Jesus, why would people be so perplexed about who he was?

When John began questioning Jesus' Identity from prison, Mathew 11:3 said, "Are you the one who is to come, or should we expect someone else? "He asked this question because he had some expectations from Jesus, who did ministry differently. That was a clear sign of his rivalry against Jesus, who came to redeem the lost sheep of Israel; he was focused to the core and did ministry in connection to God the Father. His style and approach were different because he was all for the kingdom.

How do you know when one is preaching a different gospel? Look at his approach and style of ministry. If it is not kingdom-focused, he is building a different kingdom and preaching his own message. Many have built personal empires in the name of preaching the gospel of the kingdom, a very distinct feature is in their style of messages, Christ-centered or not.

If John, the forerunner of the Messiah, had preached the gospel of the kingdom as he was anointed to preach, Jesus would not have struggled with acceptance from the people. He would not have needed to seek out his disciples himself. The disciples John prepared for himself were meant to be for Jesus if John had completed what he was supposed to do.

What am I trying to say here? Jesus, rather than moving on with ministry when he got out of the wilderness, restrained himself and went back to seek out his disciples. Jesus, after he finished from the wilderness, entered Galilee, and preached the same gospel which John was supposed to preach. Mark 1:14-15 "Jesus preaching the gospel of the Kingdom of God saying, "The time is fulfilled, and the kingdom of God is at hand, repent and receive the gospel." That is the gospel John was supposed to have preached, pointing to Jesus as the kingdom of God.

It is not as if John did not know of the gospel he was supposed to preach because he initially preached this same gospel in the early days of his ministry. "In those days ...John the Baptist was preaching in the wilderness of Judea, and he was saying "Repent... for the Kingdom of God is at hand" (Mathew 3:1-2), but he did not complete his ministry. Notice that Jesus started preaching this same gospel immediately after John was imprisoned? Mark 1:14. He waited for John to see if he could return to the course, but he did not. As a result, Jesus encountered many problems, especially from the Galilee and Judea populations, who almost killed him untimely when he told them of his true identity as the Son of God. As a result, some of the people questioned Jesus' identity in Judea, saying, "Is this not Joseph's son? (Luke 4:22).

In conclusion, the narrative of John the Baptist's ministry serves not to diminish his role as the forerunner of the Messiah but to illuminate the errors that many of us as people of God are prone to in our ministries today. We must draw wisdom from scripture as apostle Paul wisely stated, "All scripture is given by inspiration of

God, and is profitable for doctrine, for reproof, for correction, for instruction in righteousness: That the man of God may be perfect, thoroughly furnished unto all good works" (2 Timothy 3:16-17). This divine guidance is our beacon, leading us to a more perfect understanding of our ministry.

Above all, a man of God, a minister of the gospel of Jesus Christ, who comprehends his purpose and remains steadfast, should not be swayed by the perceived glory of another man or woman of God. As we have discussed in the early chapters of this book, Jesus, in John 17:1-7, demonstrated the right way to initiate and conclude a ministry successfully. Let us be resolute in our purpose, unwavering in our commitment to the gospel, and undistracted by the allure of others' glory.

Chapter Four

Validation of His True Identity
The Temptations of Jesus of Nazareth

First Temptation: Changing Stone into Bread

After enduring relentless attacks in the wilderness, Jesus found his morale at an all-time low. The purpose of these assaults from Satan was to instill doubt in his Sonship, a struggle that many of us can relate to. There are days when we are bombarded with so much that we begin to question the reality of what we've heard, wondering if it's all just self-deception. It's in these moments that our faith, steadfast and unwavering becomes our anchor, reassuring us of the truth.

At this point in Jesus' life, after he had gone through many challenges, including being sick from the bites of venomous serpents and scorpions, Satan shows up; he said to Jesus, "If you are the Son of God, tell these stones to become bread." Jesus answered, "It is written: 'Man shall not live on bread alone, but on every word that comes from the mouth of God." (Mathew 4:3).

Let me tell you what happened here, Jesus was physically looking at the stones. These thoughts were running through his head: look at you, with everything you have been through, and now you are so hungry. Are you indeed the Son of God? Let's check if you are indeed the son of God; look at these stones before you and turn them into bread.

But Jesus said to him (Satan), "Man (Jesus as a man) shall not live by bread alone, but by every word that proceeds out of the mouth of God. What word proceeded out of the Mouth of God concerning Jesus' Identity? It was that very word that Father spoke to him at baptism: "You are my son; I am well pleased with you." (Mathew 3:17). God the Father had already told Jesus to beware of anything that would challenge his identity as the true Son of God, and not participate in any act to try to prove his Sonship. Jesus in the moment of temptation, held onto the very word that proceeded out of the mouth of God, inspiring us all with his victory over doubt and temptation.

Second Temptation: Satan told Jesus to Commit Suicide

The Bible says Satan took Jesus to a very high mountain and said, "If you are the Son of God, throw yourself down. It is written: "He will command his angels concerning you, and they will lift you up in their hands so that you will not strike your foot against a stone" Jesus answered him, "It is also written: 'Do not put the Lord your God to the test.' (Mathew 4:5-8).

You know, the angels were already in the wilderness ministering to Jesus, as the Bible said, so hearing this from the devil made some sense, but the intent behind it was to get rid of Jesus before his time.

Let me tell you something that will intrigue you, by the Spirit of the Living God, I was made to understand that Satan was confused by the name Jesus. He was confused because in heaven, Jesus was known as the "WORD" and according to prophecies in Isaiah 7:14, 9:6-7, 11:2-4, the Messiah was going to be born, and his name would be called Immanuel, which means 'God with us. The name Jesus was significant as it indicated the divine nature of the Messiah, but it confused Satan because he was busy looking for someone with the specifications and the name according to Isaiah, and he got himself deceived.

The name Jesus was confusing to Satan because it wasn't prophetic. The birth and everything about the Son of God was so prophetic, except for the name Jesus. According to Isaiah, the prophetic name that the Son of God was to bear was Immanuel. When the name Jesus appeared, it confused Satan and many Jewish people until the baptism of Jesus; when the heavens opened, God the Father announced Jesus as his Son. That was when Satan appeared on the scene and tried to cut him off. Satan truly wanted to cut the Messiah off untimely to make sure he didn't save humanity. Also, he wasn't sure how Jesus would become the Messiah, so he was confused about many things concerning Jesus.

Returning to our discussion, Satan, in his deceitful nature urged Jesus the Son of God to commit Suicide. His sole intention was to eliminate Jesus, preventing him from fulfilling his role as the Messiah.

Let's examine Satan's level of deceit in the scripture he quoted in Mathew 4:5, which he twisted around. If Jesus wasn't in tune with the word, he would have fallen victim to the scheme of Satan.

Beloved, there are moments when you may feel that life is not worth living. This is a tactic the devil uses to claim lives, even those of God's children. Remember, as a child of God, you are a target of the forces of darkness. They seek to suppress or attack you, but with vigilance, you can resist their influence.

Many are falling prey to the devil's cunning schemes and manipulations, often without realizing it. The devil exploits their ignorance to strip them of what they believe they know. Let this be a reminder of our vulnerability and the need for continuous spiritual guidance.

Hosea 4:6 states, "My people are destroyed for lack of knowledge." This verse powerfully reminds us of the importance of knowledge in our spiritual journey. It's not enough to simply believe; we must also understand and be aware of the enemy's tactics. Now I am asking, whose fault is it that you do not know?

Why did Satan ask Jesus to throw himself down from a high place? Because he knows that tempting God the father would place Jesus in a place of enmity with God, where he would tempt God. Guess what? Angels are not deployed for such matters, and that's why many who throw themselves end up dead.

Satan's plan here was to kill Jesus, but since he wasn't sure how to do it, he wanted Jesus to do it himself. Jesus understood his tactics and dealt with him accordingly. You should be able to discern when the devil is debating with you concerning your right in the kingdom; his purpose is to steal, kill, or destroy (John 10:10). Don't let him.

The Scripture Satan quoted for Jesus was taken from Psalm 91: "For he will command his angels concerning you to guard you in all your ways, they will lift you up in their hands so that you will not strike your foot against a stone. He took some part of that Scripture out to suit his deceit. Many people do that today; they take a particular part of the Scripture to fit their deceitful nature.

You do not need to prove anything to Satan, see how he challenged Jesus' true identity by pounding and pushing him to obey his voice? you never follow the voice of the wicked one. He used the same tactic against the woman in the Garden of Eden; he persisted until she yielded. Satan wanted Jesus to yield to him, and many times, when Satan comes at you, he comes to confirm your true identity and what you know about yourself; this is how he defeats and deceives many.

In the world of today, Satan may not use the same tactics he used on Jesus, but he can tell you how worthless you are and how you are better off dead than alive. That's what he said to Elijah when he finished his exploits in Mount Carmel. He used Jezebel to threaten him and lied to him that he was better dead than alive. Elijah told God to kill him because his fathers, who were dead, were better than him (suicidal). The only thing was that he didn't know how to go about being dead; he requested God to kill him. (1 Kings 19:4).

In today's world, you are jeopardized if you don't know how to recognize Satan's voice. He will meet you at your weakest point because that is who he is. He did that to Jesus when he finished his fast; he was weak and hungry, and he came at him. (Mathew 4:2). And when Elijah was most vulnerable, because he had just completed a whole day crusade at mount Carmel where fire fell from heaven, he was also hungry and weak because he hadn't eaten nor rested the whole day.

Don't allow him to take advantage of you, and when you find yourself in a place of vulnerability, don't allow him to beat you up. Learn to fight back and learn the exact words that Jesus used: "It is written." This phrase, 'It is written,' is a powerful declaration of the authority and truth of God's word. When Jesus used this phrase, he was affirming the power of scripture in resisting the devil. But you must open your bible to know what is written concerning you.

Third Temptation: Satan demands a worship from Jesus

"Again, the devil took him to a very high mountain and showed him all the kingdoms of the world and their splendor. All this I will give you," he said, "if you will bow down and worship me." Jesus said to him, "Away from me, Satan! For it is written: 'Worship the Lord your God and serve him only." (Mathew 4:8-10)

You know, the heart of satanic manipulation is his ability to extort worship from man. Satan desired worship from the very beginning, and that got him kicked out of heaven. Satan hasn't changed; that desire is very much deep-rooted in him. He wants your worship, and if he must make you poor to get you to bow to his ideas, he will do it. Man is a god on the earth (Psalm 115:16), and if there is anyone who should dominate here on the earth, it is the man that God created, not Satan.

You know, the very topic we are discussing, the temptations of Jesus of Nazareth, were enumerated in the bible for a purpose: to validate that as a child of God, you must be confirmed as a true child of God. Jesus was led into the wilderness to be tempted because his identity as the son of God needed to be confirmed. The voice of the Father announced that Jesus was the Son of God, and there was no better time to validate his sonship than in wilderness. That means anytime you get approval from God, get ready to be tested and ready for validation. A time of shaking will come to remove the shakable things and cause the unshakable to remain. (Hebrews 12:27).

While writing this book, God instructed me to go on a fast for one week. During this time, God's glory was evident, and his presence was concentrated in my room for a whole week. I would wake up and start to pray, then go into writing. Sometimes, I would write for three to five hours without standing up from my location.

At the end of the seven days of prayer and fasting, I was surrounded by such an overwhelming presence of God. That night, I continued to enjoy the presence of God until I started falling asleep. In the middle of the night, I was awakened by the Spirit of God to pray, but I remained asleep because there was such a level of serenity in my environment, and I decided it was time to sleep. I woke up that morning with a vicious witchcraft attacks, I was so angry, it made me so depressed that I was tired of what I was doing. I was tired of writing, I didn't have the strength to pray, and all I wanted to do was fight, but I restrained myself.

I was so angry throughout the day that I didn't speak to anyone. But I did something, I cleaned the whole house. The energy was spent by the end of that day. It was the last day of my fast, and when it was time to break my fast, I began to worship. I forced myself into worship, and immediately I began to worship, I felt the presence of God fill my room, and I had a blast in the Holy Ghost. That's how I ended my one-week fast, victoriously.

The enemy demanded my focus; he wanted me to focus on what he was doing and nothing about God. That's another way the devil demands worship: to divert your focus from God to himself, because he knows if he can get your attention enough, then he can demand worship from you. Never give the devil your focus, he doesn't like to be ignored, and that's why he makes the most significant noise. Learn to ignore him by focusing on Christ and all the finished works of salvation; that is how you establish your victory.

After Jesus's temptations, he emerged from the wilderness and entered the synagogue. The devils whom he had defeated during his confirmation in the wilderness, cried out, acknowledging his true identity. "What do you want with us, Jesus of Nazareth? Have you come to destroy us? I know who you are—the Holy One of God!' (Mark 1:24). This recognition by the devils is a testament to Jesus's power and authority.

Jesus and the Fig Tree

The Bible tells us that after the Devil tempted Jesus in the wilderness, he left him temporarily until a more opportune time (Luke 4:13). But we never ask when this time was, when did the Devil return to Jesus? You know, the issue of Jesus and the fig tree he cursed was an exciting interaction. A fig tree that had something to say to the Messiah, what did it then say to Jesus?

First, consider the interaction between the fig tree and Jesus of Nazareth. Jesus had just finished a triumphant entry into Jerusalem before encountering the fig tree. The people celebrated him, and Hosanna was sung. People laid their garments and tree branches on the ground for his donkey to walk on, a red carpet, and a royal treatment. The Bible says they finished from the temple in the evening and then entered the next city called Bethany to pass the night. In other words, Jesus had fasted the day before he encountered this fig tree. He was busy going about his father's business, and by the time they were finished at the temple in Jerusalem, it was too late to start looking for something to eat. They spent the night in Bethany to return to Jerusalem the next day because he needed to teach in the temple.

Do you remember any other scenario like this? Yes, when Jesus finished fasting for forty days and forty nights, the Bible said he was hungry afterwards. That was when Satan tempted him to turn the stones that were before him into bread (Mathew 4:3-4).

Now, the Bible said he woke up the next morning, and was very hungry. And he saw the fig tree with leaves (a form of deceit), and he went to see if he might find something. The fig tree's conversation with Jesus is a mystery that piques our curiosity. What did the fig tree say to Jesus? This same fig tree in the Garden of Eden offered fig leaves for Adam and Eve as a cover-up and in replacement for the Glory of God that was stripped from them when they sinned. The same fig tree has a history of being possessed or manipulated. The Devil got into the fig tree and offered Adam a fake covering in replacement to the Glory of God in Eden (Genesis 3:7).

This time, guess what the Fig Tree said to Jesus? The same thing that the Devil said to him when he was hungry after his fast in the wilderness. The Devil left Jesus for a season as the Bible rightly said, then returned back in form of the Fig Tree and offered him to produce fruit from the fig tree. This is a striking parallel as it echoes the Devil's temptation in the wilderness. Ok, this is exactly what the fig tree said to Jesus, when he searched and couldn't find any fruit; "If you are the son of God, you have the ability to Fastrack the season, create fruits out of the leaves that you see" And the Bible said, Jesus answered back, cursing the fig tree (Mark 11:13-14).

If you doubt what I just said, please find out why Jesus would answer back to a standing tree if the tree hadn't said a thing to Jesus. The Bible said Jesus answering, said to it, "No man eat the fruit of thee hereafter forever" (Mark 11:15).

Hiding under an umbrella of sin, Nathaniel and the Fig Tree

The fig tree was known for its popular features in the Bible and featured in many of the events surrounding historical events in the Bible. What made the fig tree a bad tree since everything God created, after he created them, he called them good? How did the serpent get corrupted since God did not make any corrupted animal or beast? From the beginning of God's creation to the end of it, God saw and proved it to be good after each creation. When he created man, he said it was very good, which means that the creation of Man by God was certified and proved by God to be a very good thing.

The Bible says that Philip found Nathaniel under the fig tree after he had searched all over for him. Nathanial was hiding, and no one could have seen or known why he was hiding except God himself. If the Bible said Philip found him, it means Philip had searched for him for a while. Where was Nathaniel, and what was he doing under the fig tree?

He was sure to close his tracks properly to maintain his deceitful nature and his title as righteous, an Israelite in whom there is no guile. And when Jesus said, "Here indeed is an Israelite in whom there is no guile" (John 1:47), he was very sarcastic about it.

To further deepen your understanding, let's consider why Jesus said to him, "I saw you" rather than I know you? (John 1:49). Because Nathaniel's question to Jesus was, "Where do you know me from?" or rather, "How do you know me?". The Greek word "know" here is "Genosko," a knowledge that is deeper than mere knowledge, which occurs through a certain level of experience and encounter. In other words, Nathaniel was saying to Jesus, you haven't experienced me, and you are calling me by my religious title. That's why Jesus had to tell him that he saw him and what he was doing under the fig tree before Philip, who was looking all over for him, eventually found him.

If you have ever encountered God in the person of Jesus Christ, you would understand what I am about to tell you. Whenever you are conversing with Jesus as a person or with the Holy Spirit, your whole being stands and is heightened to what he is telling you. If his discussion is about a fig tree, in a split second, your entire being will experience and come to an understanding of what the discussion is all about. That happened to Nathaniel when Jesus said, "I saw you under the fig tree". Nathaniel's senses and understanding were enlightened to what Jesus had seen about him, which was a humbling moment.

The Fig Tree is very memorable; it's a tree that covered sin, and it provided shade for people who were shady and people who tried to hide from God. Adam and his wife, when they ate the fruit from the tree of knowledge of good and evil, God walked into the Garden, and they hid under the fig tree. They sewed fig leaves to cover the glory they lost by eating the fruit in the Garden. Though the Bible does not explicitly mention the name of the tree they hid under, I am telling you by Revelation that the tree they hid under was the fig tree.

If you have ever seen a fig tree, you will know that it is a tree that has the capacity to provide a covering shade under it. By the Spirit of God, I saw the fig tree as a place where the religious people sat to treat pressing issues during Jesus' time. You know, when widows presented to be helped, they were helped under the fig tree. Many people who needed to meet with the Rabbi to settle their matters met under the fig tree. In other words, the fig tree was not just a tree but a significant place where religious issues were resolved during Jesus' time, making it a crucial part of biblical history.

Jesus' profound knowledge of the fig tree, surpassing that of anyone else is truly awe-inspiring. He was aware of the unique abilities the fig tree possessed, which is why he monitored what Nathaniel did under the fig tree. It's as if God hid knowledge in the form of information in trees, and Jesus, being the Son of God, had access to this hidden knowledge. Every tree in that Garden had certain information it stored, and the fig tree was no exception.

In other words, when Jesus said, "I saw you under the fig tree," Nathaniel remembered everything that had ever happened under the fig tree. The woman caught in the "very act" (John 8:4), the one they wanted to stone, was caught under the fig tree.

How did Nathaniel move from the position of arrogance to total humility? Initially, when Philip found Nathanael, he told him about Jesus of Nazareth, which the prophets wrote about. Do you remember Nathanael's reply? He said, "Can anything good come out of Nazareth? (John 1:45). But it was a transformative moment when Jesus revealed his knowledge of Nathanael's actions under the fig tree. Nathaniel's arrogance was replaced by humility in the face of Jesus' divine knowledge.

When Jesus told Nathanael, "When you were under the fig tree, I saw you" (John 1:48), Jesus was bringing the things he had done under the fig tree to his memory. Look at it this way: Nathanael was not humbled by the statement Jesus made, what humbled him was that Jesus knew his secrets and didn't judge or expose him.

That's why Jesus said to him, you believe me because I said I saw you under the fig tree, but if you believe hereafter, you shall experience the supernatural. Jesus restrained himself from judging Nathanael and persuaded him to believe in the Kingdom of God. What humbled Nathaniel was Jesus' ability to make him remember everything he did under the fig tree, the secrets he hid from the people; that was the moment of repentance for Nathaniel. That's how the Holy Spirit brings people to their knees; he reminds them of the need for a Savior, that was the moment for Nathaniel, a moment of Grace.

Chapter Five

Jesus and the Legion (Lunatic) Demons

The revelation and knowledge of our Lord Jesus Christ and the things of God are very progressive and as the Spirit of God leads, you must follow, if not, you will be left stagnant and religious. Many have said that Jesus cast out the demon from the madman of Gadarenes, but did he really? Jesus didn't cast out these demons; he listened to them, and they negotiated with him. This stress on dealing with the demons should intrigue you about the spiritual dynamics at play.

Let's examine what truly happened here. When Jesus got to the gate of the city called Gadarene, the madman approached him and worshipped him. First, if it was truly a worship, what would you say about the next thing that came out of his mouth?

What am I trying to say here? The worship was deceptive and not a true worship. The legion demons knew who Jesus was, they had already encountered him in the sea when they tried to sink his ship in the middle of the sea. Jesus defeated them, which gave them information about who Jesus was and his abilities. They understood that it was only by God that they would be defeated, and since Jesus defeated them at sea level, it established that Jesus was of God. This emphasis on the deceptive nature of the worship should enlighten you about the importance of spiritual discernment.

To clarify what I am trying to say, let's look at the book of Mark 4:35-39; the Bible said after he was finished teaching, and as it was getting late, he told his disciples, "Let us cross over to the other side," that other side was the city of Gadarenes. While they were on the ship trying to cross over to Gadarene, remember it was Jesus's first time entering this city. He taught all day and didn't get the chance to pray up, which was his routine before he entered into any city, you take up a city spiritually before going into it physically.

When they were inside the ship crossing over, Jesus was already tired from teaching the whole day. And he took a pillow and went to the lowest part of the ship to sleep. Jesus was a hundred percent man ok? So, he was tired as a man because he worked the whole day without rest. Now, when it was time for the battle of crossing over, he picked up his pillow and decided to rest. He knew as man what he ought to have done, but as God, he also understood he had authority over his creation, and that was exactly what he did here: use his Godly authority.

As a man, Jesus felt weak in the body, and he needed to rest. While they were crossing over, the legion demons, the spirit behind the wind that influenced the storm attacked them.

Yes, you heard me right! When you hear of hurricanes, storms and other disasters, you don't see the force behind them, all you see are aftereffects. What I am saying here is that every storm of life has a driving force behind it. Hurricanes are usually given names and genders, which determine the magnitude of their damages.

In this case, the hurricane that attacked them at the middle of the sea could be called hurricane Legion, because it was the legion holding the city of Gadarenes bound that tried to prevent Jesus and his disciple from crossing over.

Jesus arose from sleep, rebuked the wind, then spoke to the sea, "Peace be still" Mark 4:39. You see, he rebuked the wind first, why? Because the force behind the stormy sea was the legion of demons influencing the wind. You don't see the wind; but there was force driving the wind, in this case, it was the legion demons. When he rebuked the demons behind the storm, he then spoke to the sea to be calm. He understood that the sea was not forcing water into the ship without a reason; it was a big warning to Jesus that something was up on the other side. The Bible said the wind ceased, and there was calm, and the next thing, they were at the gate of the city of Gadarenes.

When this madman of Gadarenes came to worship him, it was not a true worship. "For those who will worship must worship in spirit and truth (John 4:24), which did not exist in this scenario. Look at the next thing that happened while he was worshiping, he "cried with a loud voice, and said, what have I to do with thee, Jesus, thou Son of the most-high God? I adjure thee by God, that thou torment me not" Mark 5:7. This was after Jesus discerned that the worship wasn't true and tried to cast him out of the man. Immediately, Jesus sensed something was wrong and ordered the spirit out of the man, but the spirit responded by saying the above words.

Now, let's look at the meaning of what the legion spirits said to Jesus. First, he acknowledged Jesus, saying you are the Son of the Most-High, how? He had already encountered him in the sea when Jesus rebuked him. This encounter, this acknowledgment, carries a weight of significance; only the Son of the Most High could have stopped that kind of hurricane, the legion spirit whose aim was to capsize their ship.

Secondly, the legion spirit said to Jesus, "I adjure thee by God, that thou torment me not." The word adjure here is a Greek word, "Horkizo," which is from the root word "Orkizo," meaning to bring something by an oath, to put on an oath, to solemnly enjoin. The worship he gave to Jesus was to cause him to agree with him or to pursue Jesus to swear by God not to torment him. This underscores the power of worship, even from a deceptive source, to influence divine actions.

By saying this, he commanded Jesus to swear to him by Almighty God not cast him out to the wilderness. And guess what? The legion got exactly what he requested; Jesus permitted over two thousand demons to enter their chosen place, the swine.

It's clear that the legion spirits' worship was not genuine but rather deceptive. This incident taught Jesus a crucial lesson; he never negotiated with demons again throughout his ministry on earth. Despite the Bible's mention that demons would be silenced because they recognized him, this particular demon's worship, though deceptive, managed to evoke a compassionate response from Jesus. This underscores the importance of spiritual discernment and the empowering lesson of not negotiating with evil forces.

It's sobering to think that if you crave worship and the adoration of others, you may be at risk of negotiating with devils. Worship has a powerful effect, even on earthly kings, who often reciprocate adoration with favors. Let's explore further the lessons we can glean from Jesus' encounter with the legion demons.

This kind does not go except by Prayer and Fasting

The statement above was Jesus of Nazareth's response to his disciples when they asked him why they couldn't cast out the devils from the Lunatic boy.

First, let me tell you that, what I am about to say will blow your mind. I am so indebted to the Holy Spirit for the love I found in him. I can't explain why he chose to tell me these things, it overwhelms me sometimes.

Jesus was gone for six days, up in the mountain to pray. This is to tell you that Jesus was praying and fasting for those six days he was gone, how? Because his disciples were not with him to bring him food, and the Bible said he was gone for six days. Another way to know is based on his response later. While Jesus was gone for six days, his disciples were presented with a challenge: casting out a devil from a young boy. Guess what they did? they went to look for Jesus.

You remember in Mark 1:35-36 that the Bible said that Jesus would get up while it's still dark and go to a hidden place to pray. One of those days, Simon (Peter), James and John went to look for him, and when they found him, they told him that people were looking for him.

Let me reiterate that during Jesus' absence, the disciples who had been given the power to cast out demons, encountered a new and formidable challenge. A father brought a son who was possessed by a particularly powerful demon to the disciple of Jesus Christ; despite their best efforts, they were unable to cast it out. This was a learning experience for them, a lesson in the diversity and strength of evil forces.

Do you know why? Let me tell you something that will blow your mind, the demons that possessed the boy were the same level of demons that possessed that mad man of Gadarenes. Look closely at the characteristics of these demons, and how they operated. The Bible said in Mathew 17:15 that the father of this boy said to Jesus to have mercy on him for "he is a lunatic," and whenever the demons came upon him, he would tear him apart, sometimes casting him into fire and water to kill him. The same characteristics were also seen in the Madman of Gadarene; he would cut himself with stones and was often violent, and no one could restrain him (Mark 5:4-5).

The disciples of Jesus of Nazareth were faced with the same legion spirits that possessed the madman of Gadarenes, and they were not fit to cast out this level of demons, because they were not born again yet. It's worth mentioning that a legion could be as many as six thousand demons. These were also the same demons that disciplined the seven sons of Sceva in Acts 19:13-17.

This brings me to another point. Jesus had already encountered the legion spirits, but do you know what baffles me here? Jesus of Nazareth, when he was initially faced with these demons' called legion, didn't cast them out; he had mercy on them and allowed them to go into the swine, which caused further problems for the people of the city.

What am I trying to say here? Jesus didn't cast out the legion spirits from the madman of Gadarene; he allowed the demons to go where they wanted to go, which was into the swine. They, in turn, drowned the herds of swine in the sea, turned back and entered the city, and influenced the people of the city to come and cast Jesus out of the city. After Jesus had this experience, he never negotiated with nor interviewed demons. The Bible said that Jesus would forbid them to speak and cast them out, which came after his experience with devils, which possessed the madman of Gadarene.

When Jesus was faced again with the legion spirit, this time from the lunatic boy, he demonstrated his divine authority. He commanded the spirit to depart and never return. Notice what happened here? In Mark 9:20, the spirit upon seeing Jesus, immediately threw the boy into a convulsion. He fell to the ground and rolled around, foaming at the mouth.

The spirits saw Jesus and became violent. Do you know why? They remembered their encounter with Jesus at Gadarenes, and how it ended. This time, they know that Jesus will not give them any chance for negotiation. This Jesus was a different Jesus, the Jesus who had just gone through the Mount of Transfiguration. They were not by any means getting away this time.

What I am saying in essence is this, when they met Jesus at Gadarenes, he was not prepared for them. Jesus had just finished teaching sessions that lasted almost the whole day and then entered the ship with his disciples to cross over to Gadarenes.

Let me refresh your mind, when Jesus entered the ship, he took a pillow and went to sleep at the ship's lowest level. The Bible said there arose a storm against them, his disciples woke him up, and he rebuked the wind and calmed the storm, Mark 4:35-39.

The next thing that happened was entering the city gate, and the madman appeared to meet them. The legion negotiated with Jesus and got Jesus to say yes to them, entering the herds of swine. From there, they returned to the city and mobilized the people against Jesus, who was sent out of the city because he negotiated with devils he needed to cast out, Mark 5:16-17. The same way some of you are negotiating with demons you have authority over.

The Jesus who dealt with the lunatic boy, was different from the Jesus who encountered the legion at Gadarenes. He was coming from a high place, a place of power and encounters. He had a touch of heaven on him from the Mount of Transfiguration, and he had experienced the legion before, so he knew what to do with the wicked spirits. The Mount of Transfiguration was a pivotal moment that transformed Jesus, empowering him to confront the legion with confidence and authority.

Jesus cast out that deaf and dumb spirit from the boy, but what was very interesting here was, Jesus commanding the spirit not to return back to the little boy, an action which introduced a dimension in casting out demons. Let me explain further; Legions are territorial and like to return and occupy where they were sent out from. That's why they asked Jesus to permit them to go into the herds of swine in Gadarenes, so that they could turn around and return to the city. And that's exactly what they did. This time, Jesus told them to go and return no more. (Mark 9:25-26).

I am saying that the reason why Jesus told the demon spirits from the lunatic boy to come out and enter him no more, as recorded in Mark 9:25, was because the lunatic spirit, which is also the same spirit that possessed the madman of Gadarene, always like to return. That's why Jesus of Nazareth had to be specific in his instructions. Remember, Jesus once said in his teaching that when an unclean spirit is gone out of a man, he walks through dry places, seeking rest, and if he finds none, returns to his previous house where he came out...Mathew 12:43-44.

Upon further reading, you will notice Jesus' powerful command to the lunatic spirit: "Thou dumb and deaf spirit, I charge thee, come out of him, and enter no more" (Mark 9:25). The word "charge" here, as used by Jesus, is the Greek word "epitasso," meaning to command or superimpose. This time, the demons encountered Jesus' command, a form of imposition with which they could not negotiate. This was a stark contrast to their first encounter with Jesus. The first time Jesus spoke to the lunatic spirit, who later identified as a legion, he had not commanded them. He had simply told them to come out of the man, and not only that, but he also called them a different name, an unclean spirit, which was different

54

from what the demon later identified as. In other words, Jesus called the legion demons an unclean spirit, which was the wrong name, and then he told them to come out of the man. But they negotiated with Jesus and got away with it.

Look at it this way, Jesus asked the demon his name because he refused to come out and resisted him. When you are casting out demons, please make sure your word of knowledge is intact because when you call demons by different names, they detect your ignorance and give you a hard time.

Many have attempted to cast out demons for extended periods, only to find themselves unsuccessful. The key to success lies in two factors: knowing the demons by their names and ensuring your spiritual standing is secure before engaging in such a task. This spiritual stability, or right standing with Jesus, is crucial before casting out demons.

Another point worth knowing here is that, in Mark 9:25, Jesus called the lunatic spirit a "Dumb and Deaf spirit." When the boy's parent approached Jesus, he told Jesus that the boy was possessed by a dumb spirit in Mark, but Mathew called it a lunatic spirit. They are the same thing, so Jesus didn't disprove what the parent called the spirit. The parent had been to other places with the boy, trying to cure him of the evil spirits, that's why he knew the name. But, when Jesus approached the demons, he added another name to its name: "Dumb and Deaf" Jesus identified that lunatic spirit as a dumb and deaf spirit, which tells you that there are many other categories of names under the lunatic or legion spirits. That was what Jesus addressed here.

When his disciples asked him why they couldn't cast out the demons from the lunatic boy, he told them, "This kind does not go out but by prayer and fasting" (Mark 9:29). This underscores the importance of spiritual preparation in dealing with this level of demons. You must be spiritually prepared and charged in the place of prayer, not only prayer, your character must be consistent with that of the one you represent, Jesus of Nazareth. These group of demons are very violent and will always resist you if you lack the legal ground. Hence: "this kind goeth not but by prayer and fasting" (Mark 9:29).

Jesus of Nazareth: Raising the Dead

Everything Jesus did, he spoke into being before he did it. He prophesied about raising the dead before he started raising the dead. In John 5:25, Jesus said, the hour has come that the dead who can hear my voice will live again. His voice, a divine command, can bring life to the dead. According to this statement, only the dead with the ability to hear his voice, will live.

In other words, those who are dead and are also deaf or hard of hearing will not live. What am I saying here? When you try to raise the dead, the first thing to consider is their spiritual ability to 'hear' the voice of God. It's not about physical hearing but about their spiritual receptivity. This understanding empowers you to discern the crucial role of spiritual receptivity in the resurrection process. Spiritual receptivity is demonstrated in a heart that is open to God's word, a mind that is willing to understand His will, and a spirit that is ready to obey His command. Ensuring that the dead you are trying to call back to life possess this receptivity is crucial. The inability of the dead to live is not because life is denied to the dead but because the dead have a stronger impediment, something stronger than death, called spiritual deafness or hard of hearing.

The book of Romans 8:14 says, "How can they hear unless someone has preached to them? So, the dead need a special visitation called a hearing before they can live.

Jesus lifted his voice at Lazarus's tomb and cried out, "Lazarus, come forth." (John 11:43).

Jesus shouted loud enough to make sure that Lazarus could hear him. It would have been a bitter experience if Lazarus had been deaf to Jesus' voice and wouldn't have responded.

You must realize something here: Jesus had already seen Lazarus's death in John 5:25. He could see what the enemy had planned for Lazarus, and at the same time, he planned to physically defeat death by raising Lazarus to life.

According to Jesus's life and example, raising the dead involves two determinant factors. First, he saw it before it happened, meaning he was aware of that situation spiritually. Second, when he was ready to raise Lazarus from death, he raised his voice and called out his name, and Lazarus heard him and obeyed his voice.

The basic principles here were Jesus's ability to discern death and Lazarus's ability to hear the voice of the Master and respond in obedience. As I said earlier, reiterating what Jesus said in John 5:25, "verily, verily I say unto you...when the dead shall hear the voice of the Son of God: and they that hear shall live," John 5:25. The last sentence is very interesting, "they that hear shall live." I hope you can understand what I am trying to say; only those who hear his voice shall live. It then means that the ability of one being raised from death to life is depended on their ability to hear the voice of the Son of God.

Then I ask, are you trying to raise the dead? Are you the voice of God? Is Jesus speaking through you? If yes, then determine if the dead can hear the voice of Jesus Christ. When these two conditions are met, the dead shall surely live. The worst thing that can happen to the dead is to be deaf or hard of hearing.

Paul also said in Romans 8:11 that raising the dead in Christ is easier: Jesus has the keys of death, and "if the same Spirit who raised Jesus from the dead dwells in you, He that raised Him from the dead shall quicken your mortal bodies by his Spirit that dwells in you."

Paul is giving us another piece of information: the secret to raising the dead lies in the state of the spirituality of the dead. Were the people you are trying to raise from the dead believers? Did they have the Holy Ghost in them? If they did, raising them from the dead is so easy. Once their body hears the voice of God in you, they will be quickened. They will jump if you tell them to jump. It's a testament to the power of faith and the Holy Spirit. This emphasis on the power of faith and the Holy Spirit should make you feel hopeful and encouraged. The state of your spirituality is crucial in the resurrection process, but with faith and the Holy Spirit, anything is possible.

Your body has the ability to raise the dead and heal the sick. As I said, if the Spirit that raised Jesus from the dead dwells in you, He will quicken your mortal body, and your quickened mortal body can also activate whatever you desire on anyone around you. It happened to Peter, where his shadows cast on the sick, and they were healed (Acts 5:15-16), and even the dead body of Elisha was still active to the point that his bones raised the dead, 2 Kings 13:21.

Certain Species

There are certain species that cannot be raised from the dead, and if a member of your family belongs to that specie, it's not possible to raise them back to life, because they are not totally human. Jesus said to the Pharisees, you are of the devil your master, you are not of Abraham, because if you were, you would not attempt to kill me. Jesus went further to say, you cannot hear me because there is nothing in you that connects to God, that would make you hear me.

In other words, Jesus is saying that for you to hear his voice, which is the voice of the Son of God, you must belong to the Father. The seed of Abraham, and if you are not, then you belong to another specie which is the devil. (John 8:42-47).

This brings me to this conclusion, if your dead relative is a seed of the serpent, one who traded his soul with the devil, then it is impossible for them to experience salvation in form of rising from the dead. There are certain species of people called Nephilim who have fleshes, but are not human, these cannot be raised back to life once they are separated from their bodies. They cannot be reunited back to their bodies, that spirit will have to find another flesh to inhabit.

Making Disciples of all Nations

Jesus ascended into heaven, but before that, he met with his disciples in Galilee on top of a mountain. He said to them, "I have all the power both in heaven and on the earth given to me by my Father. Now, go and make disciples of all nations, baptizing them... and teach them to observe all I have taught you" (Mathew 28:18-20).

The problem is this, many who are being taught don't even know what Jesus instructed them to learn. In school you receive syllabus as a student, and it becomes a guide to what the teacher is going to base his teaching on for the semester. As Bible students, we received the Bible as a guide to what we will be taught, but unfortunately, many Bible students have no clue what the Bible says about the matters they are being taught. Hence, they have become victims of their own ignorance.

When you know what your syllabus says and are conversant with the guideline, you can easily tell when your teacher is teaching a topic that is not covered in the syllabus.

I am aware that there are many things that the scripture didn't not cover, but anything which the scripture didn't not cover often has a reference in the scripture as a guide.

There will always be a similitude of any topic God is revealing to you in the scripture.

The problem is this, many Bible students have been taught to focus on their teacher, the man of God or their pastor. The issue with that is, your teachers become a guide to your learning, therefore you are limited to only what your teacher knows.

Jesus said in Mathew 7:22-23, "Many will say to me Lord, Lord, did we not prophesy in your name, and cast out demons in your name, and did many miracles in your name? But Jesus said, I will say to them "I never knew you, away from me evil doers."

It's a dangerous thing to continue to follow a man of God and not experience the God of that man.

The statement, "I never Knew you "(Mathew 7:23), is with the Greek word "Ginosko", which frequently indicates a relationship between the person knowing and the object being known. It means that this type of knowing must come with an experience between the two; the one knowing and the one being known.

When you focus on a man of God, you just know the man, but not the God of the man. This means on that day like Jesus said, since you had not known or be known by God, you stand the chance of no place in the Kingdom of Heaven. It is a very dangerous thing, but if Jesus said it, surely, many are going to be disappointed, because they have served men on earth rather than serve God.

All I am saying is this, while you are serving your man of God, get to know his God, experience the God of the man, make sure he is serving the true God, Jesus Christ the Messiah. Because on that day, you can't plead ignorance as a defense.

Be wise as Serpents!

Jesus said, "...Be wise as serpents and harmless as doves," when he sent his disciples out to witness; because he knew the adversary they were about to encounter, Mathew 10:16. The point here is this, don't ever consider Satan a fool; he is the old serpent, which means he is privy to a certain level of knowledge.

The old serpent is generational; he was there when your great-grandfathers negotiated out of ignorance. The old weapon he used against your fathers is the same weapon he will use against you, and if you overcome, he will try other weapons. But the good news is this; we are of God and have overcome the world, 1 John 4:4. This victory over Satan should empower us and give us hope in our spiritual journey.

The Devil tried some of his tactics with Jesus, he disguised himself and asked him to turn the stone into bread to prove he was the Son of God. But Jesus knew it wasn't about the stone or bread but who the master here is, whose voice is superior? Are you going to obey the voice of an old serpent because you want to prove that you are the Son of God? or will you stand complete in God, because he already approved of you and doesn't need you to try to listen to the old serpent.

You know Jesus' temptations were challenges to prove his Sonship. The Devil wanted Jesus to obey him, and that was the only way Jesus could prove to Satan that He (Jesus) was the True Son of God. The first temptation was to turn stones into bread, the second was to jump from the temple and be saved by angels, and the third was to worship Satan in exchange for all the kingdoms of the world.

Let me conclude by saying that the Devil is still that old serpent; he is wise at deceit but very harmful because his very purpose is to steal, kill, and destroy. When you are dealing with Satan, be it known that he is not a fool, and when you give him a chance, he will steal a generation, you, your children's future, and that of their children.

Give God a chance, a relationship that can help you know who you are in him, so you don't fall into the hands of that old serpent when he beckons at you. A strong relationship with God is your shield, your protection against the temptations of the Devil. Because if he tempted Jesus, you are surely going to be tempted.

Chapter Six

The Spirit of Antichrist

The spirit of Antichrist is an expression of Satan in human form; just like Jesus was the expression of God the Father in bodily form. This spirit has been looking for a physical body to manifest, like God manifested in the form of Jesus Christ.

Antichrist, as a spirit has always been around; he was here even before Jesus was born. This spirit manifested in the form of Herod, who killed all the toddlers born during the period when Jesus was born. This spirit of the Antichrist also manifested during the time of John the Baptist, who entered Herodias and requested the head of John the Baptist on a platter.

Jesus entered the world through natural birth and did many things as a man and God in the flesh. Since the devil likes to imitate God, he is also looking to be born into this world and manifest the way Jesus manifested, but he will be crushed in the end. Apostle Paul told the Thessalonians in 2 Thessalonians 2:3-4, that the end will not come until the Antichrist, whom he called the man of sin and son of perdition, is revealed.

At this moment, I am convinced that the Antichrist has already been born and is biding his time to manifest. This man, the Antichrist, will likely manifest around the same age range as Jesus of Nazareth.

Lucifer being a deceiver and aspiring to be like the Most High, was locked in a state where sin was found in him. As Ezekiel 28:15 rightly said, he has remained the same since sin was found in him. Once sin was found in him, he was cast out in that very form, a sinful nature, without redemption. In other words, everything about the Antichrist will be a total show of sinful desires and deceits.

Let me share with you this insight: Lucifer, the son of the morning, was around the same age as Jesus when sin was found in him. Jesus made a crucial statement, "the prince of this world cometh, looked in me, and found nothing in me." Do you know why? Because Jesus, at that point, was at the same age when sin was found in Lucifer. This very information was what he was seeking from the woman in the Garden of Eden. When he said to the woman, "Has God said you should not eat of the trees of the garden?" he was cunningly trying to extract the knowledge she had about the trees of the garden. Unfortunately for him, the woman was not ready to disclose certain information God gave her. The woman was a custodian of many other information about other trees in the garden, a topic for another day.

What I am saying, in essence is this; the man antichrist will come from a group of young people, will mingle with the young minds, and then be presented to the world as a solution to the problems of this world. Just as we notice the uprising from the youthful population, their ability to rule their world and be in control has increased, and the Antichrist will take advantage of that to try to manifest.

When he physically manifests on earth and is known as the solution to the world's problems, he will relocate to Jerusalem and try to rule from there. He will try to live as Jesus lived, have disciples like Jesus did, and have people who will work with him; they are being groomed already. As I said, Satan likes to replicate whatever God does; he is going to choose his own disciples around the same age as the twelve disciples of Jesus Christ.

The spirit called Antichrist entered Judas Iscariot, who then betrayed Jesus. Judas was not redeemed or couldn't be redeemed because once this spirit enters a person, that person becomes irredeemable. This spirit enters people who position themselves to be used, and once an Antichrist spirit possesses a person and uses the person, that person's life cannot be redeemed, just as the devil cannot be redeemed.

The Antichrist spirit almost overtook another disciple of Jesus, but Jesus intervened. Remember Peter? Jesus warned him that the devil desired him, but he also assured Peter that he had already prayed for him (Luke 22:31). This incident shows the power of prayer in resisting the influence of the Antichrist spirit.

The same Peter was called Satan by Jesus when he tried to stop him from the way of the cross. The point is this: the devil can easily use anyone who positions themselves to be used. Anyone who succeeds in being used by the spirit of the Antichrist gets a place in hell; this person cannot be redeemed. This same spirit used Pharaoh against the people of God in Egypt, this spirit holds people of God in captivity and tries to prevent the manifestation of Jesus Christ through his people.

Why Judas wasn't Redeemed

The spirit called Antichrist as I said, existed in the world even before Jesus was born. This spirit resists and denies Christ. It is a spiritual force that opposes the teachings, influence, and manifestation of Jesus in the flesh. This spirit is very deadly because once it enters a person, the person is done with salvation. Therefore, there is no redemption for this person.

As I said earlier, the spirit of the Antichrist was in the world before Jesus Christ manifested physically. But you may argue why the Antichrist existed before Christ. The reason is that after the serpent was cursed in the garden, he was promised that the woman's seed would bruise its head (Genesis 3:15). Satan did not take that lightly, he understood that God does not make empty promises, and he had been preparing for it. How? By designing schemes to make sure God's promise to him was aborted. Satan has promised to prevent the liberty and the dominion of man, and he had to come up with something that will prevent God's salvation from manifesting. He monitored and aided the killing of some of the prophets of old, then eventually the killing of Jesus. All the people, measures, and avenues he used in prosecuting and killing the children of God, including the prophets, were under the undue spiritual influence called the Antichrist.

Whenever you see yourself constantly trying to prevent or resist the manifestation of salvation, and Jesus Christ physically, you stand the danger of this spirit getting hold of you. John made it more explicit when he warned believers to be aware of this spirit because it is already in manifestation, he advised us to judge well by discerning the spirits we believe, 1 John 4:1-3.

Judas, in other words, tried multiple times and things to stop Jesus or limit him on the earth, to the point of becoming a conduit for the Devil by giving him a chance to enter him.

The first thing he did wrong was not arguing with Mary Magdalen about giving or worshiping Jesus in the way she did; the first thing he did wrong was stealing from the church pocket. Judas was the accountant of Jesus' ministry and was jealous of how much people donated to support the gospel of Jesus. The Bible says Jesus' fame went abroad (locally and internationally) (Mark 1:28, Mathew 4:24). Judas was Jesus's cousin, he could not stand the spreading fame and the monetary contributions flowing into the ministry, so he became envious and jealous, and stealing from the ministry's account became his enterprise.

Judas told Mary that the gift she had given Jesus was too much for him, but Jesus corrected him and did not rebuke him publicly. He gave him multiple chances to change. Jesus said something remarkable here: "Let her alone; she is anticipating and preparing for the day of my burial (John 12:4-6).

In other words, Judas was trying to prevent the burial process of Jesus Christ, without his burial, he would not have risen from the dead to bring salvation to man. Judas loved money, the very reason he sold Jesus was because he was jealous of him, and hatred manifested (antichrist spirit) through him.

When you look at the world today, you see how people treat the name Jesus Christ in disdain, the hatred boils with anger, spilling over whenever that name is mentioned publicly, all because of the influence of this same spirit called the Antichrist. What I am saying is this; whenever you see an uprising and hatred manifesting against a people because they identify with the manifestation of Jesus Christ physically, it is the spirit of the Antichrist at work.

The most appropriate reason why Judas Iscariot was not redeemed was not because he killed himself; it was because he died outside Jesus. He separated from Jesus and submitted to the Devil before his death. In other words, he sold his soul to the Devil. The same sin many are committing today, especially certain groups. They develop hatred for Jesus, then move towards Satan, and align with him against Jesus and against anything that manifests Jesus physically (flesh).

Peter and Satan

Jesus said to Peter, "Simon, Simon, behold the devil hath desired to have you, that he may sift you as wheat, but I have prayed for you, that thy faith fails not..." Luke 22:31-32

Why was Satan desirous of Peter? Because he had Christ revealed and because he hates revelation. He also considered the disciples who would be used to betray Jesus of Nazareth. Peter was his first choice, so he considered Peter, but Judas fell for it because he loved money and was greedy.

Greed, a dangerous sin, opens one up for many disastrous encounters, and can lead to many dangerous sins including murder. It is a destructive force that can ruin lives and relationships.

Those consumed by greed are perpetually driven to acquire more. It is this insatiable desire that the devil exploits and focuses on. The devil's sin was that of insatiable greed. Never content with what he had, he always desired more. Even when given territories to rule over, he remained unsatisfied. The anointing he received as Lucifer, magnified the greed which he became by desires. He wanted to be like the Most High, and to be a master over the stars of God. This desire for power and superiority led to his downfall, as he was cast out of heaven for his pride and rebellion.

Looking at Peter, who also exhibited certain traits of trying to hinder Christ from manifestation at one point. Jesus called him Satan because it was the Antichrist spirit that tried to manifest through Peter. The Bible says that after Jesus had told them the kind of death he would die, Peter took him aside and started to rebuke him. The word rebuke is a Greek word "epitiman" it's the same word as pressing, casting out. The same word that Jesus used to rebuke devils, Mathew 16:21-23.

Peter was trying to hinder the very purpose for which Jesus came to the earth. Remember Jesus telling Peter that the devil had tried to destroy him, but because He (Jesus) had prayed for him; he told him to remember his brothers (fellow disciples) (Luke 22:31). Satan had eyes on Peter to use him against Jesus, but Judas fell into that slot.

Did you know that the devil was anointed from the beginning of his ministry? That is why he is referred to as the anointed Cherub who covered. In a natural sense, Cherubs are Angels who stand and cover grounds for God. However, in Lucifer's case, he was given a special anointing called the 'Mimshack anointing '. This anointing enabled him to perform a unique role that normal cherubs could not perform.

Therefore, when the chief angel, Michael, contended with Satan over Moses's body, he said to him, "The LORD rebuke thee Satan" (Jude 1:9). He said that to him because, given the anointing Satan was endowed with, only the LORD could rebuke him at that point. Michael, often referred to as an archangel, is a significant figure in the Bible, known for his role in spiritual warfare and protection.

Lucifer's anointing influenced the territories he was supposed to cover, the earth and part of heaven. Have you ever wondered why Lucifer convinced one-third of the angels to accompany him? These angels were part of the territories he was covering. That's why he was called the anointed Cherub that covered. He was empowered (anointed) to cover territories, including parts of heaven and the earth.

When you observe the devil's influence over the earth and some part of heaven (the second heaven), it is due to his anointing. This anointing, which he corrupted by 'trafficking, 'was not taken from him. Here 'trafficking' refers to the misuse or corruption of the anointing, leading to its perversion and the spread of evil influence.

As I mentioned earlier, only the LORD could rebuke the devil before the arrival of Jesus Christ.

After Jesus' manifestation, following his forty-day fast in the wilderness, his first action was physically rebuking the devil. This act of rebuking was a reclaiming of authority over him. The authority Adam had given to him in the Garden of Eden when he sinned was part of the authority Jesus contended with him for. The devil was trying to convince Jesus that he owned the entire kingdom of the world. At that point, he had influence over the whole earth.

What Satan took from Adam in the Garden was a key of influence called dominion over all the earth. When Satan was cast out of heaven, at the time he rebelled against God, the key to dominion was taken from him, but his anointed, which was corrupted by trafficking (Ezekiel 28:18), was not taken from him. So, he had influence still with him, but not the key to dominion.

It was the key to dominion that gave him access to appear before the presence of God, and when he took that key from Adam, he gained access back to the presence of God. In other words, Adam gave Satan control over humanity to rule over him and humanity. But when Jesus came, he had to take the key, which was dominion over the earth and the heaven. Thus, he said all power in heaven and the earth has been given unto me…" (Mathew 28:18). The Greek word used here is "exousia," which is the same word as authority, capacity, ability, jurisdiction, etc.

In essence, when Jesus faced the temptation in the wilderness, it was a battle for dominion, authority, and jurisdiction over what Adam had lost when he sinned in the Garden. Jesus, being without sin, was able to physically rebuke the devil. When he said, 'Get thee behind me, Satan' (Mathew 4:10), he was reclaiming the authority Adam had lost to Satan by triumphing over sin. The devil had said to

Jesus, 'Look at all the kingdoms of the world, if you fall and worship me, I will give you the glory and all this authority (the same Greek word Exousia), Luke 4:5, for it is all mine, it was given to me, and whoever I will, I can give it.'

It means that what happened in the Garden of Eden was partly about worship. When Adam ate the fruit, he (bowed) worshipped the devil by giving him access to the Garden. So, when he approached Jesus, it was also about worship. That is why he first told him to turn stone into bread, meaning to eat what he was offering him. Jesus responded, "Man shall not live by bread alone, but by every word that proceeds out of the mouth of God" (Mathew 4:4). What Jesus was telling him here was, even though bread is important, man cannot live by it alone, but by every word that comes out of the mouth of God. Which means that you live by God's directions and commands. Obeying the words coming from Satan is like switching his authority and obeying Satan rather than God.

Afterwards, Jesus was able to rebuke Satan, and when he left the wilderness, he took that authority with him. He then started casting out the devils. Prior to this, no one in the flesh was able to cast out demons. The reason the chief angel Michael said the LORD rebuke you Satan, was because of this anointing and the key to dominion he took from Adam. It then means that Adam could have casted him out even in the Garden.

What I am saying is this, Satan was barred from the Mountain of the LORD, a place of divine presence and authority, as mentioned in Ezekiel 28: 16. He negotiated with the woman at the garden and gained another access. When the children of God gathered in the book of Job 1:6, Satan also came into the mount of the LORD with the access he gained from Adam and Eve. (Sin is usually denies you access to God but gives Satan an easy access into your life).

Before the death of Jesus Christ on the cross, Satan held a certain level of power over man. Jesus referred to him as the ruler of this world (John 14:30), indicating that the access he took from Adam and Eve was in the form of authority to rule the world. However, Jesus publicly humiliated him, triumphing over him (Colossians 2:15). This victory over Satan by Jesus should invoke a sense of triumph and victory in us, knowing that we are on the winning side.

The Seed of The Serpent

Have you ever asked yourself who the seed of the serpent is? In the book of Genesis chapter 3:15, God told the serpent, the deceiver, that there will be an enmity between him and the woman, his seed, and her seed. This means that there will be a problem anywhere they see each other. Also, anywhere your seed (serpent) encounters the seed of the woman, there will be a log ahead. Biblically, we know that the seed of the woman is Jesus, and we who confess Jesus are also by inheritance part of that seed.

Something that is baffling is that we walk around with this prophecy over our heads, being fulfilled right before our eyes, and we never bother to ask these questions; Who is the seed of the serpent? Are they among us as well? Are they people who live in our societies? Some of them are members of our households, who are there to negotiate their course so the external ones can have easy access to our families.

Look deeply into what's happening worldwide, you will find these broods of vipers, as Jesus would call them (Matthew 23:33). People who walk around like humans but are not humans because they have serpentine blood flowing through them. How do people who are humans cut other humans in pieces like animal pieces? They are the natural seed of the serpent and their generation. Look closely;

you will see their attributes, they don't differentiate who they kill, they just don't kill their kind.

People You Should Not Pray For

There are people around you that you shouldn't pray for or preach to because it will be a waste of time. I am not the one saying this; if you open your Bible, you will understand it properly. You wonder why, no matter the amount of prayer on the heads of specific individuals, they remain bad like the devil? It's because nothing in them could make them repent, there is no space for repentance.

Look at the conversation Jesus had with some of them in John 8:31-33. Jesus was about to make them his disciples, and he suddenly realized there was a mixture of different kinds, a different seed altogether. This group of men claimed they were Abraham's seed, but Jesus said to them if you were Abraham's seed, you would behave differently; you would believe in me and not try to kill me. John 8:39-44. The mere fact that you are trying to kill me is the proof that you are of a different kind; you are the seed of the serpent, Jesus said.

When you see people who try to kill you because you profess Christ and confess Jesus, it's an indication that they are a brood of vipers. It will be a waste of time for you to start praying for them to repent and give their lives to Christ, because they will never do that.

Do you know why? Every human has a part of them that can easily be transformed and renewed. When they are not humans, you don't expect them to have a place in them for salvation.

What am I saying? Look at what Jesus said in John 8: 44-47. Jesus told them they were of their Father, the devil, meaning they were of a different seed altogether, and if they were of God, they would have received his word, his teachings. In other words, if that Godly-given conscience were in them, they would have received the word and been saved.

Next time, you must pray for someone for salvation and ensure they are salvageable and can be redeemed. Jesus gave us a perfect example when he prayed for his disciples in the book of John. Not only did Jesus pray for his disciples to the Father, but he also prayed for those who would come to believe in His name through the gospel preached by his disciples. Jesus said, "I am not praying for the World, but for those you have given me" John 17:6-20. In other words, next time you pray for people, be specific to get an answer from God.

It's important to be aware that there are people who will never repent, not because God hates them, but because they are not human. They are merely acting like humans on earth. Satan's body was destroyed when he sinned and was cast out of heaven, so he operates on earth by possessing earthen bodies. Praying for these people is like praying for the devil to repent and receive Jesus Christ, which will never happen. This understanding should enlighten us about the futility of praying for the wrong people.

When you see wickedness in action as a person before you pray for them to change, make sure that they are human beings because only natural humans can repent, those whose names are written in the Book of Life. Anyone whose name is not written in the Book of Life will never go to heaven and cannot, therefore, they cannot receive Jesus Christ as their Lord and Savior.

In addition, when you go out for evangelism, pray for guidance from the Holy Ghost and let him direct your footsteps to the right people.

Chapter Seven

The Mark of the Beast

This chapter is significant because it discusses the same quest that Lucifer nursed, which took him down from his position. He said, "I will go up above the stars of God and become like the Most High God." Here, the 'stars of God' refer to the people under his authority. Lucifer desired to rule over them as God does over his creation.

There is a portion of man where God established for himself; Lucifer desired to rule the people of God from there. He wanted to replace God in his creation. That's why once you receive the mark called the mark of the beast, there is no redemption for you; can't repent or seek forgiveness or give yourself to God, because that aspect of you where Mercy is received is blocked off, and you can't even seek for Mercy. At that point, your conscience is dead to anything concerning God and humanity.

In the case of the mark of the beast, a concept mentioned in the Book of Revelation, it symbolizes allegiance to Satan. Whoever is convinced to accept this mark, whether through technological means or otherwise, essentially pledges their loyalty to Satan. This act allows Satan to take control of their soul which controls the spirit towards Satan, usurping the place where God should rightfully be, and ruling over their lives.

The Mark of the Beast is the DNA of Satan, the Luciferian distorted DNA that he received when sin was found in him. He was the one who corrupted his DNA by the multitude of his merchanting with his anointing and gifts, as rightfully stated in Ezekiel 28.

You know there is a place where the Holy Spirit comes to convict you of sin; your conscience, after you receive this mark, which is the DNA of Satan, your conscience is blocked off, so you won't have a conscience. You, therefore, cannot seek anything apart from worshiping the beast.

God occupies a position in every man who enters the Earth; John referred to Jesus as the true light that lights every man who enters the world (John 1:9). John is saying here when he described Jesus based on the revelation, he had about him, that he is that true light, which lights every man who enters the world via natural birth. Which means there are other kinds of lights or appearances of lights but are false). Everyone born into this world has a spirit in them, referred to as a candlestick of the LORD in Proverbs 20:27, and a light through which the Lord searches the whole personality of that man.

What I am saying here is, regardless of agreeing with this fact or not, every man born into the world has a recognition of their existence by God Almighty. And that part of them that makes God aware of them is the light (spirit)in them, which they received from Jesus the true light. Jesus is the one who is the beginning of the creation of God; he was not created all things were created and originated from him (John 1:3). In other words, it is an ignorant thing to claim that you exist independently or apart from God.

The entire explanation above is to lead you to the point I am trying to make; there is a place in man, called his spirit, where God sits as a guide to his life. A man feels a void when he is not born again and will continue to wander until he finds that completion in God. Only Jesus Christ can fill that void, without him, the search to fill this void will persist.

Apostle Paul made a remarkable statement in Colossians 2:10: "You are complete in him, which is the head of all principality and power."

Man's struggle after Adam's sin in the Garden of Eden is one that we can all empathize with. But Jesus referred to as the last Adam, came to reconcile man back to his original place, the place of communion with God (2 Corinth 5:18).

Having said that, I want to remind you of the significance of being born again. When a man is reconciled to God through Jesus Christ, he is born again. This man has a renewed spirit from the contamination that happened when Adam sinned. The man's spirit becomes renewed and has God sitting at the center of that spirit. This transformation is profound and enlightening.

Now, do you know what Lucifer craved before his fall? He envied God, wanted to become like him, and planned it, accordingly, leading to his fall.

Let me make it more transparent; when Lucifer said in his heart, "I will ascend into heaven, I will exalt my throne above the stars of God, I will also sit upon the mount of the congregation, in the sides of the north: I will ascend above the heights of the clouds, I will be like the Most High." Isaiah 14:13-14, he understood very well what he wanted; he wasn't playing with words.

First, Lucifer said he would ascend into heaven, which means he was not in heaven; he was on the earth ruling among the stars of God. Even though he was given charge over the territory called Earth and had a place in Eden, that was not enough; he still wanted to be God to those he was assigned to lead. Look at it this way, he was given a territory called Earth, and there were people who existed on the Earth called the stars of God. In the Earth, there was also a garden called Eden, where God lodges when he visits the Earth.

Lucifer was assigned to take care of that garden, and as an anointed Cherub, his role was to cover that Earth and its inhabitants. This sheds light on his responsibilities and the extent of his fall.

Routinely, Lucifer would visit the Mount of the LORD, which Ezekiel mentioned in Chapter 28:14 as the Holy Mount of fire, to report unto God Almighty about the fairings of the people he guarded. Not that God who is omniscience did not know what was happening on the Earth, if not, how would he have known Lucifer planned the coup?

Lucifer while in the process of being in command, and because of the wisdom and beauty he was created with, he became proud, his heart was lifted, and he started thinking of having a throne in heaven also. Rather than being where he was positioned on earth, he wanted to become a god to the stars of God and to be lord over them. He wanted to implement his thoughts, which led to him being cast out of heaven into the earth.

Jesus said I beheld Satan fall like lightning from heaven, meaning he was thrown out of heaven with his evil conceit, Luke 10:18. It means he was going to implement his thoughts to put into full practice his plan to be the Most High. That's what he was in heaven to do. That's why the Bible said that he fell with one-third of the angels, the stars of God. What does this mean to you? It means he was already able to convince these angels and was working towards his goal when he was cast out of heaven, (Revelation 12:4,9).

Back to the topic of discussion, what Lucifer did to Adam and Eve was what he wanted to do in heaven. He deceived them into submitting to him, and he became a god unto them. That's why he is called the god of this world (2 Corinth 4:4). This is what Lucifer now known as Satan, is doing to many today, becoming a god unto them.

When that purpose is achieved, a person dies to their conscience; that aspect of them that feels guilty when a wrong is done, that aspect of them that feels the pain of others or has empathy or compassion, the soul of this person dies to righteousness. This person now can easily watch others feel pain without remorse, can easily watch people die and blood wasted without any feeling of guilt whatsoever.

The part of them that feels mercy and wants to give it back is no longer active, or better to say, is dead and cannot be revived because Satan now sits there permanently. A person is said to have sold their soul to the devil. It's like a total exchange of ownership by the devil.

There are many today who find themselves in this category; you will never see them feel bad about their decision. Not because they don't want to, but because that place or ability to feel bad is deleted from them, and they will never feel sorry or wrong about taking another life. Some of them do things that are so wicked to the natural mind and feel normal about it. Because the point of righteousness is not anywhere near, they have been bought, and no negotiation.

There is also something Satan is trying to do now; he is using various agents and avenues to create awareness or recruit many who will mistakenly take the mark. He is doing this because many have been evangelized about the mark of the beast, and he is trying different avenues and using governmental agencies to achieve this aim. He wants to get to the point where people can easily succumb and freely receive the mark of the beast without knowing it. If it takes the alteration of the human genome, he is willing to do that. But God, through man, is also aware of his devices, and the whole world is watching.

As a person, as long as you still have that ability to feel sorry and repent of evil deeds, you are safe; it means God can still reach you, but be careful because once you continue in sin, it gets to the point where your conscience is seared, sin becomes a normal lifestyle for you, it leads you to the point of no return. Apostle Paul calls it a reprobate mind (Romans 1:28). It means you have no acknowledgment of who God is and have chosen to live your life in sin; God gives up on you at this point. Your name gets removed from the Book of Life, and even though you are living, God sees you as dead and separated from him, Revelation 3:5.

Chapter Eight

Lucifer the Anointed Cherub
What he has against the Church of Jesus Christ

Lucifer was fashioned with different kinds of precious and beautiful stones on earth when he was created. This is described in Ezekiel 28:13, which lists the precious stones that Lucifer was made with. And when you read further, it tells you that he was perfect on the day he was created. A man who was made in such perfection, what could have gone wrong?

Out of God's goodness and mercy, he gives freedom to everyone he created. There is a level of freedom in his righteousness; the freedom you enjoy must be in righteousness, not vice versa. Whenever you want total freedom, go deep into God's righteousness; that's where complete freedom resides. It means that there is no freedom in sin, which is what happened to Lucifer. He moved from freedom in righteousness to corruption, which came from disobedience to the God who offered him freedom.

The day Lucifer was created with all those precious stones, something called fire was also placed inside him. This 'fire' is a metaphor for God's control over Lucifer. God put it there to keep Lucifer in check; he was the light bearer, and that light was also ignited by fire. Have you ever seen electricity catch fire? Yes, even though it gives light, it can spark fire and burn physically when something goes wrong with that electric line.

That was the part of Lucifer he didn't know about. He thought he knew everything, which is his own ignorance; he is still that way to this day. He is still going around believing he is very intelligent, to the point of knowing and calculating God's movement.

Don't get me wrong, Lucifer was created in perfection, and he had a level of wisdom given to him, which he corrupted (Ezekiel 28:16-17). In other words, the wisdom he now has is corrupt, and he uses it as a destructive weapon. It is called the wisdom of this world.

As I was saying, the very thing placed inside of him that made him shine as light was also an antidote to his unruly behavior. But he didn't know that, if not, he wouldn't have tried to become the most high.

On the day he rebelled and then attempted the coup in heaven, it was called iniquity, and that happened because of his merchandising with his anointing. This 'merchandising with his anointing' refers to Lucifer's misuse of the power and authority given to him by God. Then fire came from within him and devoured his physical body. He was reduced to ashes. Ezekiel 28:18

Man as a living Soul

The word of God said in Genesis 2:7, after God formed man from the dust of the earth, he breathed the breath of Life into his nostrils, and that made man a living soul. In other words, what made man a living soul was the breath of Life, which God almighty breathed into his nostrils. This 'living soul' is a combination of the physical body and the immaterial spirit. The soul is the seat of emotions, desires, and intellect, while the spirit is the part of us that connects with God. It is the soul that houses the spirit of a man. And if you ever need to find the position of a human spirit, you visit the soul, the site where Life lies.

It also means that as a spiritual being living in a body which has a soul, your spirit has to be revived by your soul to function properly. This revival is not a physical action, but a spiritual one. It involves aligning your soul with the will of God, allowing your spirit to be energized and guided by the Holy Spirit.

You see, to be able to see spiritually with the eyes of your spirit, the soul that houses your spirit has to give you that ability to receive sight. I am saying that for your spirit to see things and understand things spiritually, your soul has to make way for the spirit to manifest.

It's crucial to understand that it's your soul that can limit your spirit from seeing and manifesting. Recognizing and overcoming these limitations is a key step in your spiritual journey.

Your soul, represented by your mind, plays a significant role in decoding spiritual things. But to truly perceive spiritual matters, you need to transition from being a soulish person to a spiritual person. This transformation is not just a change in perception, but a profound shift in your spiritual journey.

When the Bible says that Jesus opened their understanding (Luke 24:45), it means that their minds were blocked, and the light was occluded from shining into their souls to give understanding to their spirits about spiritual matters.

Before Jesus opened their understanding or the eyes of their spirits, something had put a lock on it. That something is usually sin, which is the devil's tool to block our understanding and spiritual perception. This realization should instill in us the need for spiritual vigilance and the importance of resisting the devil's influence.

Lucifer was called a light bearer, and when he fell, he was called the prince of darkness. This means Lucifer, who is represented by sin, is responsible for blinding people's minds or understanding (2 Corinthians 4:4). He does that to prevent them from gaining access to the truth and, thus, salvation.

The Anointing Upon
The Reason Many will go to Hell

The anointing that comes upon you as a man called by God is for service. This anointing is what the people around you need. It comes upon you because of their hunger and demands. This anointing is specifically given to you to serve the population, the people you are called to serve. This anointing is for service: the people around you need the services you are anointed to provide.

Lucifer, who later became the devil or Satan, was given a population to cover and was given this anointing. That is why he is called the anointed Cherub that covereth. The book of Ezekiel 28:14 KJV reads, "Thou art the anointed Cherub that covereth." Other translations read differently. The anointed Cherub called Lucifer is still the anointed Cherub that covereth; he still has that same anointing that he received from God, because "The gifts and the calling of God are without repentance" Romans 11:29.

If the Bible tells you this is the situation, that's what it is. The same reason a man who God calls could continue to sin and still function under the anointing to heal people afterward. People would see the anointing move whenever this man rises, and that's where the confusion is; the anointing he received does not go away, but he can carry the same anointing into hell.

As I said, Lucifer received a covering anointing because he had a job on Earth. He was situated in Eden to cover that location and the Earth's surroundings.

Have you ever wondered why the Bible says the serpents beguiled the woman (Genesis 3)? This is because the serpent, a beast in the Garden, was first corrupted by the devil, who was also in the Garden.

Ok, look at it this way: if the Bible said that the gifts and the calling are without repentance, and Lucifer was called to cover the Garden of Eden (Ezekiel 28: 13) and other locations on Earth, why do you think he shouldn't be at the Garden and also the Earth? The stones God used to create Lucifer were from Eden, he felt more comfortable in Eden than in any other place. This is why the anointing does not scare him, he carries an anointing, a very heavy one. It is also the same reason he can attend your church services unless you ban him. Just to advance in this knowledge, Lucifer is not afraid of the anointing, he has one, a great one. If he was afraid of the anointing, he wouldn't have attempted to have a conversation with Jesus, after he was anointed with the Holy Ghost. The Bible said after Jesus was baptized, heavens opened, and the Holy Ghost descended upon him like a dove, (Matthew 3:16). What happened here was the anointing of Jesus of Nazareth by God the father. Guess what happened afterwards, the devil went after him, bragged to Jesus how he(devil) owns the World and everything in it, and on his ability to give it to whoever he wills, Luke 4:5-6.

Also, in the book of Job1:6, When the sons of God gathered together, Satan also appeared with them. Do you know why? Satan loves the anointing, he can relate, because he is anointed. Everything he knew until his fall was a heavy weight of the presence of God and the anointing. What scares him is righteousness, which is the reason he was kicked out of the Mount of the Lord.

The reason I gave you the above information is to confirm to you that the devil is not afraid of your anointing, what he is afraid of is your righteousness, because that is what he is lacking.

The only reason he should not have been in Eden, was because Adam was given dominion on earth, and a special task concerning the Garden in Eden. The same way man has authority on earth today, but still allows Satan to interfere. The point is this, Adam allowed him access into the Garden out of his own negligence.

Lucifer was also given access to the Mount of God, which was filled with stones of fire, which is the only place he was banished from because God could not withstand sin. Lucifer was alienated from the Mount of God, Ezekiel 28:16. When he was banished from appearing before God, he had his place on Earth and the Garden because those were his primary locations.

But I want you to see something dangerous here that many tend to ignore; Lucifer was banished because sin was found in him (Ezekiel 28:15). What is interesting here is that Lucifer was created in the perfection of beauty and every other thing, including wisdom. God gave him a little piece of himself, which is what all the men of God also receive from God.

That little piece of God called the anointing was what other cherubs didn't have; hence, he is called the anointed Cherub. Not that other angels of God are not anointed, they just have different heavenly bodies which distinguishes them from other creations of God. Lucifer was created differently. As an angel of God, he was separated and anointed for a purpose. That was the last time God anointed an angel with the same anointing because Lucifer rebelled.

As I said, sin was found in Lucifer, but sin didn't just appear; there were things he did that contributed to the birth of something called sin. The book of Ezekiel 28:16-17 tells us how he arrived in sin. It reads, "By the multitude of your merchandise, they filled the midst of thee with violence, and thou hast sinned ..."

First, he discovered something about the anointing he received. It was for the need of the locations he covered. There were demands being placed on him, just as many children of God go to their man of God to receive from them.

Once Lucifer discovered that he could give what the people were demanding, he discovered he was a bridge, a gap between God and the population he was covering. Then, as mentioned by Ezekiel 28:16, he began to also make demands from the people. This was the origin of his merchant business.

Lucifer discovered he could also place demands on the people for the anointing he received freely from God, and it became a trade by barter, hence the origin of "Trade By barter". If you need my anointing, bring something to me, if you need healing bring a seed and put it on my altar.

Have you not noticed that the seed on the altar works? Yes, it does, but whatever you receive does not last because this kind of merchandising originated from Lucifer. He is the originator of trade by barter, which many men of God practice today.

While performing his coverage to the people, Lucifer demanded worship from them in return for the provision of services. As if what he got in return wasn't enough, he took it to the highest level, wanting to become God or replace God in the lives of those he covered. Watch: this is a very subtle sin, and it is very tricky. Yes, it is essential to honor people that God has used to bless your life, but worship is what God will not share with anyone; that is the place of God, and many receive it comfortably.

In contrasting and discouraging this kind of trade, Jesus said to his disciples when he gave them a taste of this anointing, he charged them against the sin of merchanting with the anointing; he said in Mathew 10:7-8 "As you go preach this message... heal the sick, raise the dead, cleanse the lepers, drive out demons. Freely you have received; freely you shall give."

Jesus specifically instructed his disciples not to take anything from the people before providing them with these services. This was a reminder that the anointing they received was not for personal gain, but for the benefit of the people.

Lucifer engaged in many exploitations and negotiations with the people he was covering, and when he was highly successful at this (merchanting), he began to conceive of sin. He changed the focus to himself, began to see himself in his array and glorious reign over the people, and then came sin.

What was then his sin? This is a cautionary warning of the dire consequences of exploiting the anointing. Since he could negotiate with the people he was assigned to serve and receive services from them, he decided he could also be god to them. Remember I said earlier when I started that the anointing that comes upon you as a man or woman of God is for servicing the needs of the people; you serve the people and not the other way around. But the problem is this, when the man of God who is a servant begins to demand services from the people they were meant to serve, then merchanting begins.

Lucifer, after he discovered this secret, decided he could not just receive services from the people, he could also become a god unto them; this version of being a god unto the stars of God got him into satanism, hence: Isaiah 14:13-14 "I will ascend to the heavens; I will raise my throne above the stars of God. I will sit on the Mount of assembly... I will be like the Most High."

Do you remember I said he was banished from the Mount of the Lord? Because he had access to the Mount of the Lord, which is where the general assembly meetings are held. After his imagination, he attempted what he said in his heart, and that's when he was banished from that Mount, his access was taken away from him.

The anointing is very dangerous, it has the ability to bless you as a man of God and the ability to destroy you as well. As a man of God, you feel blessed to see and hear all the testimonies of the people, the deliverances, and the miracles they received by believing in the anointing upon your life. You feel blessed as a man of God because anytime people in need come to you, and they demand this anointing, they actually receive whatever they desire.

This is why when the woman with the issue of blood pressed through the crowd saying in her heart, "if I may but touch the hem of his garment, I shall be whole," Mathew 9:21. She received because her needs drew out her healing from Jesus of Nazareth. Remember, the anointing is not for you as a man of God, but for the people you are covering. This is what it means exactly: as many as those within your covering who recognize their need and believe you carry an answer to their problems will also receive whatever they desire.

But don't forget that there were times when Jesus of Nazareth was approached by people outside his constituency, and they made a demand also on this anointing, even though he had originally said no, the people's faith pulled out of him what they needed. Like in the case of the woman who made a demand concerning her daughter, whom the devil vexed. She came and knelt before Jesus (a form of recognition and worship) and said, "Lord, help me!" But Jesus replied, "it is not right to take the children's bread and toss it to the dogs." Mathew 15:25-26.

Here is the catch: even though Jesus called her child the dog, which today would make many furious and lash back at Jesus disrespectfully, this woman was wise and knew that her child's healing depended on this moment, so she persevered in faith.

First, this woman, in receiving from Jesus, acknowledged what Jesus said because he was right. The anointing Jesus was carrying was for his people at that moment. He was sent to the household of Israel, not to everyone (Matthew 15:24). But the woman told Jesus there could be an exception to this rule. Do you know what this woman told Jesus here? She told Jesus he had control over this anointing, which was the very truth, and that he could also extend his coverage.

This woman, an Assyrian outside Jewish territory, heard all the beautiful works of Jesus. She decided she could cash in for her child in faith. Regardless of what name you would call her, she was going to pull out her child's deliverance from Jesus. The Lord told her, "O woman, your faith is great! Let it be done for you as you desire." Matthew 15:28. The Bible recorded that her daughter was healed from that very hour. What an incredible miracle!

The anointing is given to you for the people, but you, as a man of God, have control over it, which is why people misuse it. It's a gift given to you for the people, but as a carrier of that gift, you control what you do with it, a total freedom that can only be experienced in Christ.

The emphasis is on the control a man of God has over the anointing he receives from God for the people. It was up to Jesus to say no to this woman or perhaps ask her to bring money since she was outside his assigned territory, or maybe to bring her body, which many men of God do today. But He, the master, the Lord full of compassion, was touched by this woman's faith, and he released that anointing, which healed the woman's daughter.

There is also a similar case in the Bible, the centurion, in which the disciples pleaded with Jesus to attend to his needs. According to them, he loved the Jewish people and built a synagogue for the Jewish people. Jesus agreed to go and heal his servant. The man marveled and told them to tell Jesus that he was not worthy to entertain him under his roof, but would instead he spoke a word, Luke 7:3-9. Jesus, in turn, said, "...I tell you; I have not seen faith like this in all Israel" (Luke 7:9).

Remember I said Jesus' covering was only limited to Jews? This was before his death, and he was restricted because he must die in Jerusalem. If he died outside Jerusalem, the prophecy would not be complete.

All of this narration of Jesus and the people who pulled whatever they needed out of his anointing was to bring you to the point of emphasis that I made earlier; You are in control, in charge of the anointing upon you for the people. You are in control of it, but you are also accountable for whatever you do with it or how you use it.

If you look closely at Jesus's life, you will see that he made many references to the Father, his source. Jesus's ability to control and contain this anointing, which destroyed Lucifer and has destroyed many men of God, was his continuous dependence and relationship with the Father. Jesus understood the secret to maintaining a successful ministry and finishing well; he maintained a good and constant relationship with God the Father, the source of his anointing.

When a man of God who received something from God and decide to function independently of God, who is not attached to his gifts, whatever you receive could destroy you.

Jesus, throughout the scripture, would send his disciples away and move into a secluded place to bond and be taught of his Father, the source of what he received at baptism, Luke 3:22. He continued to say, I do what I see my Father do, I say what I hear my Father say, making references to the source of his anointing, John 5:19. But many men of God today, take God out of the equation and put themselves in the center which was where Lucifer wanted to be, and this is why they are destroyed.

Man was created to seek God, to be fulfilled and sustained by a relationship with God alone. In other words, man is a seeker of God. It does not matter where you place man, he will seek God. Some seek him differently from others. Some seek in the caves; some seek in trees, earth, graven images, etc. that's why many religions exist today. Because when God created man in his image as requested by Lucifer (he wanted to be like God), God decided to place that vacuum in man called the soul where the thirst for the creator exists. Many still feel empty without the true God, regardless of how wealthy, beautiful, etc.

Consider the tree the serpent tempted the woman within the Garden. It bore the fruit of the knowledge of good and evil. Lucifer, in his curiosity, defied the divine command and partook of this forbidden fruit. His disobedience not only led to his fall but also to the perpetual nature of sin.

The reason the serpent asked the woman, "...Did God say you should not eat of every tree of the Garden?" Genesis 3:1. Because that's the instruction he was given, not to eat of the tree of the Garden. The Garden belonged to God including the trees; prior to Adam no one was allowed to eat of the fruit of the trees in that Garden. It was the Garden of the Lord (Ezekiel 28:13), but Lucifer was given access, just like Adam and the woman. God told Adam he could eat from all the trees except the fruit from the tree of knowledge of good and evil, which was different from Lucifer's instruction. God allowed Adam to eat from all the trees because Lucifer fell after he was told not to eat from any of the trees. Not only did he eat from the trees, but he also ate the forbidden fruit.

Lucifer also traded with the fruits of the Tree of the Garden. He gave some angels some to eat, and that was his purchasing power. That was how he convinced some of them who rebelled with him. And that's how some wicked angels were able to access the dark knowledge they taught man after the fall of Adam.

This means that the violent trading that Ezekiel referred to, was the purchasing power of offering the people he governed the fruit of the tree of knowledge of good and evil, and then rivalry ensued in him.

Lucifer, having tasted the depth of wickedness, sought to corrupt the woman. He deceived her with the promise of enlightenment, saying, "You shall not surely die, for God knows ... your eyes will be opened, and you will be like gods, knowing good and evil" (Genesis 3:4-5). His words were a cunning ploy to lead her astray.

As I mentioned earlier, man's quest for God will persist until the void in his soul is filled by a genuine relationship with God through Jesus Christ. This truth was amplified in John 14:6, when Jesus, in response to Thomas's query about the Kingdom, declared, "I am the way, the truth, and the life; no one comes to the Father except through me." This is not a mere statement but a profound truth of utmost importance, non-negotiable.

Many react negatively to Jesus's name because they know that what Jesus said is the absolute truth and cannot be negotiated. If you want a genuine relationship with the Father, you must come through Jesus of Nazareth, not through any other relation, head, or person.

The misuse of the anointing, a divine empowerment given by God to his chosen servants, will send so many to hell. When God created man, he didn't make him to be dominated by anyone other than God. Man is only created to become God's subject and not the subject of his fellow man.

Whenever a man is made to be subjected to another man, the word slavery ensues. No man is created or born into slavery, but people make their fellow men and subject them to slavery.

Whenever a man of God puts himself in God's place in anyone's life, that man becomes an object of worship and relinquishes his original place as a man to a god. This is a Luciferian act, an act that mirrors Lucifer's rebellion against God and will attract Lucifer's judgment. It's a sin of rebellion, which is also considered witchcraft in the eyes of God.

Many people practice witchcraft and subject the people of God to wicked attacks just so they can have dominion over them. The anointing they received to help the people has been turned into a tool of witchcraft and manipulations against the same people they are here to help.

Having known all the above information about you, it is very important to know that Lucifer has one major thing against the church of Jesus Christ, against the man created in the image and after the likeness of God: Envy! The fact that Lucifer fell from a height because he had desired to be like God in a very wrong way, and to see that the same thing he desired was what man became on earth is devastating. This is in line with the biblical account of Lucifer's fall in Isaiah 14:12-15. Lucifer has a special hatred for the man that God created in his image, because man was given the image of God and the abilities to be like God on earth.

Lucifer has made a vow that he will perpetually resist the man and the God man represents on earth. But he does not have the authority to do that. Man, in his divine image and with the authority bestowed upon him, has authority over Lucifer and all the works of his hands. Therefore, what he uses against the people of God is ignorance, a tool that loses its power in the face of our divine authority, revelation, and the true knowledge of God; you know yourself and understand your authority over Satan by your true knowledge of God.

Chapter Nine

Stand Complete
You are the head of All Principality and Power

Apostle Paul, in his message to the Colossians, shared a crucial insight that is paramount to your identity as victorious Christians. Understanding the context, Colossae was a small town in South Asian Minor, known for its production of red wool clothing, the colosseum. This unique trade was their trademark, much like your unique identity in Christ is yours. Today, Colossae would be in Southeastern Turkey.

That was just a brief history so that you will understand where Paul was coming from. It was also known or said that during this time, there were people who had contrary opinions about the death and resurrection of Jesus Christ, so they were trying to convince the people that Jesus was not really God in the flesh.

Apostle Paul started by warning them to pay attention very well, lest they be deceived by human philosophies in Colossians 2:8. He was telling them that people are going to try to make them think otherwise about their position in Christ Jesus. He called it vain deceit and the rudiments of men and the world. Theologically, what I am about to tell you is not justifiable, but biblically, it is provable.

Apostle Paul told them to follow the tradition of Christ and not the other way around. The tradition after Christ is this: You received Christ, walk in him with the same faith used when you received him. Colossians 2:6. Paul went further to say that they should strive to take root in Christ, because what he would tell them is only for those who have taken root or are deeply rooted in Christ.

The same apostle said in Galatians 4:1 that as long as an heir is a child, he will remain a servant even though he is the lord of all. In other words, even though he has that kingship in him, as a child, he does not know the things that are due to him because he is a child and lacks the capacity to rule.

Apostle Paul's message to the Colossians is clear: don't let anyone deceive you about your true identity in Christ. Stand firm in this truth. When you stand complete in Christ, you hold authority over all principalities and powers. This is your empowerment, your confidence.

Here's a crucial point that may seem dangerous at first glance. Theologically speaking, it might raise some questions. This is why I started by telling you that you might encounter some challenges here. It's important to approach this with caution and a discerning spirit.

Apostle Paul's teaching in the sixth verse illustrated the importance of walking and being deeply rooted in Jesus Christ, which will cause them to be established in his name. Walking in Jesus means living a life that reflects his teachings and character, while being deeply rooted in him involves a strong, unwavering faith and a deep understanding of his word. And being established in that name brings what Paul would call being complete in Him (Jesus Christ).

Apostle Paul says that once you stand complete in Jesus Christ, your standing complete is what all principality and power bow to.

It makes you the head of all principality and power when you stand complete in Jesus Christ. You become a high standard because when you stand complete in him, you walk, live, and have your entire being in him. You become his hands, feet, voice, and full representation on earth, which is the head of all principality and power.

But you know, the first time the Holy Spirit told me this, I thought I was just hearing voices, but he led me back to that Scripture, and I read it the way Paul wrote it. And he opened my eyes or rather the eyes of my understanding to see it as it was written in KJV. It reads, "And ye are complete in him, WHICH is the head of all principality and power" Colossians 2:10. What does that mean to you? It reads which is, why didn't it say who is?

When others started interpreting it, they couldn't imagine that man would become the head of all principality and power, so they offered their opinions and interpretations. Yes, I argued with the Holy Spirit, how can this be? We have always been told that Jesus is the head of all principality and power, which is not out of place. Still, the Holy Spirit is saying here that Paul wrote what he wrote because it is possible to be a complete representation of Jesus Christ on the earth. And as a representative of him, you will also command the same respect as though he were present, because he is. The Holy Spirit plays a crucial role in guiding us into all truth (John 16:13) and helping us understand the deep things of God (1 Corinthians 2:10).

To further deepen my understanding of this topic, the Holy Spirit took me to Ephesians 2:6, which says that the Father has raised us up with Jesus Christ and made us sit together in heavenly places in Christ Jesus.

And he asked me, do you believe that you are seated in heaven now, and in Christ Jesus? I said yes, even though it doesn't appear that way at this point. He asked me where I was seated; I said I am seated at the right hand of God the Father, far above all principality and power, Ephesians 1:21. He said, if you believe you are seated in him, then where is Jesus seated? He is seated at the right hand of God the Father, far above all principality and power and might and dominion. This means that spiritually, we are already in a position of authority and victory, even if it may not be physically evident.

Why do you struggle when Paul declares that you are complete in Christ, and because of this completeness, you have authority over all principality and power?

That's why I started by saying that if you are a child, you are like a servant. In other words, because you do not know who you are yet, you are being toasted up and down by these principalities and powers that are supposed to be under your feet.

You know the most dangerous aspect of it is in the process of standing complete. It's a battle you must face because those principalities and powers, the might, and the dominions, don't want you to know who you are. And they are going to do everything possible to keep you down and make sure you remain a child. This battle is a spiritual one, where the forces of darkness will try to undermine your understanding of your identity in Christ and keep you in a state of spiritual immaturity.

The battle is about focusing on the image of Jesus Christ and being transformed into his image from one level of Glory to another. Our spiritual growth and victory come from aligning our thoughts, actions, and beliefs with those of Jesus, thereby becoming more like Him in character and authority. This is the battle you must fight, and through it, you will emerge victorious.

The Holy Spirit also asked me, why did John say; "as he is, so are we in this world" (John 4:17). If we agree that Jesus is seated far above all principality and power and might and dominion, then John is saying that we, too, are seated above all principality and power in this world.

Child of God, strive to get to know Jesus, once you discover him, you will discover yourself.

Paul told the people of God to walk in Christ the same way they received him; you received him by faith and walk in him through faith. It would be best if you made a conscious effort to keep this faith in an activated form.

Another controversial statement as revealed by the Holy Ghost is in Isaiah 59:19. It reads, "So shall they fear the name of the Lord from the west (America, Europe, and other western countries) and his Glory (man in the image of God) from the rising of the sun (where does the sun rise from? The east: China, Asia, and Africa), that when the enemy would come in like a storm (remember where it will come from? From the west and the east) then the Spirit of the Lord will raise a standard (man made in the image of God), against him.

This confirms what Apostle Paul said in Colossians 2:10: You are complete in him, which is the head of all principalities and powers. You are the standard that the Holy Ghost will raise up against these principalities and powers. It is the man made in the image of God, the complete man who has dominion over the devil and his wickedness. That's why he fights so much to ensure that you do not know who you are; the day you see this light, you will mess him up.

You Are the Temple of the Holy Ghost

In the old covenant, the ark held immense significance in the temple. It was the most potent possession of the Israelites, often called the

God of Israel. The awe it inspired was a testament to the power of God's protection. Whenever the ark was present, especially in battle, the God of Israel was believed to be present; the people understood that the Israelites had victory even before the battle started because their God would be fighting for them.

It is this same reason that made Barak, the king, hire Ballam, the Prophet, to curse the people of God because he heard many things that their God did with other nations where they were coming from. He was afraid, so he wanted the prophet to curse them (witchcraft) because he realized that cursed people don't manifest God.

Ballam was a hungry prophet. Though he was interested in working for God, he was so hungry for the reward of silver and gold that the king of Moab promised him that he got greedy and distracted.

This king understood that the only way to make God look away from his people is when they are under a curse or spell. Subsequently, the seer Balaam tried but was restrained because he couldn't curse a man under a blessing. Child of God, you are either blessed or cursed; there are no in-betweens. This means that you are either in a state of blessing, where God's favor and protection are upon you, or you are in a curse, outside of God's favor and protection. When you are under a blessing, people may try to curse you, but they will end up blessing you. No curse can stick to you, only blessings.

King Barak took it upon himself and decided the people of God were his enemy, without any encounter or interaction with them. He didn't like them, he just decided they were his enemy. Numbers 24:10.

There are people who look at you, and just because you look good or too beautiful, they are afraid of who you are becoming. They decide that what will make them happy is to see you go down, and if possible, disappear from the surface of the earth. To them, your existence is their nightmare. You are not quite where God is taking you, but they say they cannot be alive to see you get there.

The king of Moab Barak saw the people of God for the first time coming through after he watched what they did to Sihon, king of Amorites. Sihon was a powerful king who fortified himself with a great army and fortified his city with great walls. This king Sihon had before fought against Moab and took all their land. When the king of Moab saw that the Israelites had defeated them and taken over the Amorites, he was challenged and fearful. Out of his fear, he decided that Israel was his enemy. It was his own decision that Israel was going to be his enemy, and in order to protect himself, he was going to curse them.

Ballam got crafty with the people of God after he tried to curse them, and it didn't work. His witchcraft mode kicked in, and he advised the king that the only way to bring the people under a curse was to make the same God who blessed them also curse them. He told him that if the people can be lured into Idolatry, they will automatically fall into a curse (Revelation 2:14).

Balaam practiced both divination and witchcraft; he used seducing spirits to influence his subjects. Numbers 24:1 The Bible says he did not turn to divination like other times, meaning he had the ability to do one or the other. The spirit of God only came on him when he decided not to use divination, Numbers 24:3

His witchcraft caused him to advise King Barak to release his adulterous women into the camp of the people of God. These 'adulterous women' were not only involved in physical adultery but also spiritual adultery, as they led the people of God away from their faith. The people didn't go after the women initially, the women came into their camp and defiled them, luring the people of

God away from God, who fell to their witchcraft by whoring after the strange women and their God Baal of Peor. It's more like the witchcraft used by Delila on Sampson.

As a result, 24000 people of God died because of the plague God released against them. You would think since the people were bewitched and lured into this act of ignorance, God should have just spared them, but God doesn't stand Idolatry; it was the first thing he commanded them to avoid. This first commandment still stands today because when Jesus, who did not abolish the law and the prophets came, he fulfilled the laws of Moses; he made it complete.

Jesus said the first commandment is to "Love the Lord your God with all your heart and with all your soul and with all your mind" (Matthew 22:37). God still hates Idolatry today, so we will examine it deeply. However, as a reminder, you belong to God and should treat your body as a sacred object of worship. If you understand this principle, you will manage yourself well, knowing that as a temple of God; there are certain things you will not allow and will not be associated with.

Idolatry

Idolatry is a form of worship, where an image is made and placed on an altar where sacrifices are made. Self-worship is a form of idolatry; it is the most popular form of idolatry that exists today on the earth. Here, an image is formed in your mind or your imagination; then, you proceed with worship, which can present in the form of what you say with your mouth or what you do. Here, the altar is your heart; that's where the object of worship is placed. God said, these people worship me with their mouth, but their heart is very far from me, (Isaiah 29:13), because for a true worship to occur, the heart must be involved. In Idolatry, the heart and action have to agree; if not, worship is not complete.

Jesus also reiterated it in the book of Mathew 15:8-9, when he was teaching them about religion and idolatry. The heart is not just a place of worship, it is the altar of the human body, the sacred ground where our deepest allegiances are formed, and our truest worship is revealed.

Self-worship is the root of all the little groups of associations rampantly taking over people's lives, which carries grave consequences. Whenever a person or group of people arise in an uproar to talk solely about themselves independent of God, look deeply; self-worship is involved. This self-centeredness can lead to spiritual destruction and separation from God.

We discussed Lucifer and his fall in detail in the prior chapter; it will be important to highlight under this topic that he is the originator of self-worship. Isaiah states that Lucifer said in his heart "I will ascend into heaven, I will exalt my throne above the stars of God, I will also sit upon the Mount of the congregation, in the side of the North. I will ascend above the heights of the clouds; I will be like the Most High" Isaiah 14:13-14.

When you examine the above scripture well, you will notice one common thing: the word "I WILL," which is significant for self-actualization and the origin of self-worship. All Lucifer focused on was himself, and that focus was achieved in his heart, which was his altar of worship. In other words, Lucifer, first of all, worshiped himself before desiring to make himself an object of worship. This is typical of many who have demanded worship from others; the focus is on themselves first before desiring it from others.

Whenever you pay obeisance to a man with an image of him in your heart, and you proceed to say to him that without you, life would have amounted to nothing, then you have created an idol of that man.

Look at what happened to Herod of Agrippa; the Bible put it there so that you would not say that the New Testament didn't address idolatry. Making a man an object of worship was addressed in the New Testament.

In the book of Acts 12:21-23, King Herod arrayed himself in royal apparel and addressed the people. While he was addressing them, they kept chanting and praising him, "the voice of God, the voice of God," and an angel sent by God smote him.

What was interesting here? He didn't demand any worship from the people, but because the devil knew that was what his heart desired, he gave it to him. Would you not argue that God should have punished the people worshiping the king rather than the king himself? The Bible said he was killed because he didn't give the glory to God.

In other words, when men flatter you and pay obeisance to you, what you do is to either stop it which is the best option or direct it back to God. This redirection is not just a suggestion, it is a necessity. He sees your heart whenever people begin to make an image (idol) of you, and he waits to see the response you give. That determines the judgment, and it's a matter of eternal significance.

Religion
A form of Idolatry

Religion is a form of idolatry where the focus shifts from the true God to the rituals and idols of the religion. Jesus wasn't popular with the religious group. They hated him for not being religious. In fact, the primary reason they offered him to be crucified rather than Barabbas was because he called himself a son of God, and that made him equal to God. John 5:18. To the religious mind, that was offensive. Just the same way what I am about to say to you will offend the religious mind terribly; it was a direct challenge to their traditional beliefs and practices.

The religious minds offered Jesus up to be killed rather than deal with the truth. Do you know what Jesus was trying to say to the religious Pharisees? You don't need to follow religious rituals to get to the father. He told them to get to the Father, "I am the way," John 14:6. In other words if you must get to the Father (which is a big deal), you must come through me. It was sacrilegious to hear that Mary's son, whose Father fixes cabinets (carpentry), says he is the son of Almighty God.

They were so offended because they were ignorantly religious; their minds were blinded by their rituals. They were so religious and ignorant that they didn't understand the scrolls they carried around because inside those scrolls were prophecies regarding the birth of Jesus and how God was to send his son to redeem them back to himself. But you know a religious mind is a perilous place, almost as deadly as witchcraft.

Religion binds: it removes your eyes from the truth and keeps you focused on mundane things, on rituals that have no way of helping you; it's just a tool the devil uses to hold people in captivity.

Jesus came, died, and said, you have free access to the Father; all you need is to confess that Jesus is Lord and believe that the Father (God) raised him from the dead, and then you have access to the Father, who is the source of eternal life. But religion tells you that Jesus's option is too good to be true, you need to go through rituals, calling on dead images and people to help you get to the Father.

Religion says you must carry some rituals and call on idols and images to intercede for you. But if you were not a religious fanatic, you would one day read the book of Jeremiah 7:17-20 and Chapter

44:8-19, Where God rebuked Israel for burning incense to an idol called the Queen of Heaven. You have the potential for understanding and discernment, to question and seek the truth beyond the rituals. Imagine the freedom that comes from this understanding, the liberation from the constraints of religious dogma.

If you were not blinded by religion, you would one day ask yourself why you go into a church and shrine dedicated to the Queen of Heaven, when God said that the Queen of Heaven is an idol. If you were free, you would one day ask yourself, where and what is the origin of the idol Queen of heaven and other idols you believe in? Was she one of those idols the people carried from Egypt because they were born into it? Why was the first commandment the people received, targeted towards Idolatry? Was it because they were born into Idolatry and engraved into the idols in Egypt? Questioning these practices is not a sign of disrespect but rather a sign of engagement in your faith. Idolatry replaces the worship of the true God; it takes your focus off the only True God and fixes your eyes on the idol of your choice.

If you are not blinded by religion and if you desire to know the truth, your eyes will be opened to it. When the devil wants to ruin your life, he will keep you from knowing the truth because he is the father of all lies and deception. But remember, seeking the truth is empowering; it puts you in control of your spiritual journey.

God Seeks True Worshiper

There are certain people on earth whom God will naturally seek their presence. These individuals are unique to the earth or any environment where they find themselves. Their presence is where God wants to be, for something about them pleases God. It's a privilege to be among these chosen ones.

God called King David the man after his own heart, but before that, Samuel the prophet said to King Saul, your kingdom would have been established, but now it's taken away from you because you have done foolishly, 1 Samuel 13:13-14. Prophet Samuel didn't stop there; he also said, "God hath sought for him a man after his own heart..." This is where the focus is, but not many people know it. God had to seek after David before he determined him to be the man after his own heart, a man who would fulfill the desires of God's heart, not his selfish heart desires.

What makes a man or woman unique on earth is their spiritual connection and ability to see or hear God's heart and bring it forward. The book of 1 Corinthians 2:11 says, "Who knows the thoughts of God but the Spirit of God?" The Spirit of God has the ability to reveal God's thoughts to us as his children. This spiritual connection is what sets them apart.

What I am trying to say is this: There are certain people for whom God seeks their presence because their presence is the presence of God in any environment. God knows that they will represent his interests and course when found anywhere on earth. These are the kind that the Father seeks; they represent true worship to God.

David, as a shepherd boy, had a unique ability to bring God's presence to an environment. He achieved this through "true worship," the kind that is done in spirit and truth. David could make God come into a city or an environment even though God had departed from that city.

When King Saul had a spiritual problem, his servant offered him some advice: "An evil spirit from God troubles you." Send for a man who can harp well..." 1 Samuel 16:16. This servant knew something that his master didn't quite know well, the ability of an anointed musician to bring the presence of God to an environment, by removing the devil from that environment.

David was sought because another servant of the King had experienced him and could testify that God was with him. David's ability to cure the King of his devil was not because he could play the harp well but because he knew how to physically bring God into an environment.

Moses understood what God's physical presence would do to an environment and negotiated well with God about leading them physically.

Certain rare and precious individuals have the unique ability to usher in God's presence and transform the atmosphere. These chosen ones not only bring God into an environment but also sustain that divine presence. As a true worshiper, you are part of this select group, representing a heavenly atmosphere wherever you go. Learn to embody this transformative power by seeking a deeper relationship with God, and as a true carrier of God's atmosphere.

Jesus and the Woman at the Well

The profound encounter of Jesus and the woman at the well, as narrated in John 4, is a pivotal moment in the biblical narrative. In a surprising turn of events, Jesus chose to journey through Samaria. This unexpected decision, as he was on his way to Galilee, piques our curiosity. Why did he choose this route? The answer lies in his divine knowledge of the woman he was about to meet.

Spiritually, Jesus would have encountered this woman and known that she was John the Baptist of Samaria. Why did Jesus go through Samaria at that particular hour when the woman usually came to draw water from the well? He may have encountered this particular woman and also studied her a bit. Do you think it's the first time Jesus went through Samaria to Galilee? Did Jesus see this woman before, even from afar? Peradventure, Jesus would have heard her story because words get around. He decided to meet with this woman on that same day since he already knew when she came to draw water. Jesus would have wondered before this meeting why a young lady like her would prefer to draw water on a hot afternoon rather than the cool of the day.

The sixth hour was around noon when the woman usually came to draw water from the well. This woman was so popular that she avoided everyone and avoided the times when regular people would go to draw water, which would be first thing in the morning and the cool of the evening.

The woman at Jacob's well, whose name was withheld, was a celebrity and a very bad one; she wouldn't want to be seen around other ladies who probably had issues with her for her kind of lifestyle. She took people's husbands away from them and hid them at her house.

But Jesus needed to meet with her, so when he got to the well, though the Bible said he was weary, he decided to rest there. Why didn't he rest before getting to that well at noon, since he was tired? At the same time, why send his disciples away to go and buy food? A very significant and suspicious act. Perhaps he knew how his disciples' religious minds would react to it, he didn't need their judgmental minds.

First, the disciples were shocked that even Jesus was in close proximity to this woman, the Bible said they marveled at it. John 4:27. Why did they marvel? Because Jesus is a messiah, and Jewish; how can a Jewish messiah be talking to a sinful Samaritan woman closely?

This woman's suitable attribute was her ability to fish men and keep them at her house. What did Jesus see that qualified her as one of his disciples? She was able to disciple the men of Samaria for Jesus; she was good at talking to the men.

When Jesus convinced her that he was the Messiah, she left to gather the men, who listened to her and believed in Jesus after they heard him speak because a woman discipled them within hours.

Jesus told the woman at Jacob's well, "For the time is coming, and now it is, for the true worshippers shall worship the Father in spirit and in truth, for Father seeks after such to worship him." Jesus knew at what hour the woman would be there and when God desired a tool to surface for true worship. This woman at Jacob's well with all the bad images she was labelled with, later became the most influential disciple mentioned in the Bible, though people in her community saw a woman with marital instability and other relationship problem, Jesus saw a true worshipper.

Mary the mother of Jesus: The influence she had on Jesus

When Mary declared, 'The wine is finished,' she was not just pointing out a shortage. She was revealing her profound understanding of the child she carried and gave birth to. Mary's unique revelation of God during her pregnancy was not that of a typical mother. She saw in her child not just a son but a master of the universe, a God, a miracle worker, a Lord, and a Savior.

Mary's understanding of her child as the Messiah was not a mere human insight. It was a knowledge tested and confirmed by the Holy Ghost. Mary, pregnant by the Holy Ghost and bearing the child of the Holy Ghost, was undoubtedly filled with the Holy Ghost. Let me tell you that not only was the baby Jesus encapsulated by the Holy Ghost, but Mary was also.

Angel Gabriel, the great messenger of God, said to Mary, "The Holy Ghost shall come upon you. The power of the Highest shall overshadow you" (Luke 1:35). Two things to know here: First, the Holy Ghost coming upon Mary was a supernatural ability being released to her to house and manifest as the mother of Jesus, and Second, the Power of the Highest, which is also another level of manifestation of God the Father.

In other words, God the Father, the Son (Jesus), and the Holy Ghost were all manifested through Mary. For that ability to manifest into God in human flesh, the three personal manifestations of God were all displayed to Mary.

When Mary's natural became supernatural, she also received much of God's revelation through that. To confirm what I am saying, let's look at what happened when Mary packed up her things and ran to visit her cousin Elizabeth. The Bible says that when Elizabeth heard Mary's voice or greetings, the baby in her womb jumped or leaped, and Elizabeth was filled with the Holy Ghost.

Now let me ask you, where did the Holy Ghost that filled Elizabeth come from? Jesus was a spoken word at that time. When Mary entered the house of Zacharias, Elizabeth's husband, and she spoke the word as a greeting, the baby leaped (that leaping is a result of being filled with the Holy Spirit). It did not end there; the mother of John the Baptist, who was that baby in the womb, also got filled with the Holy Spirit.

What do people do when they are filled with the Holy Spirit? They begin to manifest. Part of that manifestation was also recorded in Luke 1: 42. She spoke out in a loud voice (when the Holy Ghost Manifest, there is a loudness to his manifestation). What did she say when she spoke in a loud voice? She prophesied, a form of confirmation of the message Angel Gabriel brought to Mary. In case Mary had a bit of a doubt later in her pregnancy, she got a confirmation from her cousin Elizabeth. Luke 1:42-45.

The purpose of going through the information above is to bring you to the knowledge that I want you to have, the knowledge that will transform your life as a child of God. The Holy Ghost can manifest through you any day and anytime. Even before Jesus died and was resurrected, the Holy Ghost was there, and now, He is in full manifestation.

Mary turned around at a wedding party, and he found Jesus, who at this time was a full-grown man in his early thirties. Mary knowing the timing that was given to him by God, looked at Jesus and said to him, "There is no more wine" (John 2:3).

Why would Mary turn to face her son Jesus, who was invited to a wedding ceremony, and say to him, "There is no more wine," if she didn't understand the timing?

Mary was under the influence of the Holy Ghost and understood perfectly well the timing of God's revealed events. At this point, she was moved to influence her biological son, who is God in the flesh, to start manifesting as God.

She said to him, "There is no more wine! This child of mine who is supposed to be also my Lord and my savior, when are you going to manifest?". According to the Jewish calendar, at this age, Jesus should have already been married and had many children, but none of those had happened, and Mary understood purposefully well. He is not married and does not have children, but at least he has to manifest because he is becoming too old for Mary's liking.

Jesus, being fully aware of his mother's reverence and respect for him, understood the deeper meaning behind her words. The same woman who had always protected and guided him, knowing that

CHIOMA AFOKE

he had a destiny to fulfill, prompted Jesus to manifest his divine abilities, indicating that the time was ripe.

Jesus responded, 'What is my concern if the wine is finished? I am just a guest like everyone else.' Mary's faith and determination did not waver. She continued to believe in her son's abilities and instructed his disciples to heed his prompting. Even though Jesus told her that his time had not fully come, Mary told Jesus that the time was now.

The Greek word used by Jesus is "hora," which also means season. Jesus said to his mother, "This is not yet my season," but his mother said to his disciples, "Whatever he tells you, do it."

What unfolded here was a powerful manifestation of the Holy Ghost upon Mary, Jesus's mother. The Holy Ghost moved her to activate Jesus's time and season, demonstrating the immense power and influence of the Holy Spirit.

Guess what? Jesus manifested, and the people experienced a miracle. That miracle strengthened Jesus's faith, whose supernatural abilities were turned loose.

Do you remember that I said earlier that Elizabeth's child was filled with Joy, which is also a manifestation of the Holy Ghost? This only happened because Mary activated the spoken word as a greeting. When Mary spoke, Elizabeth and her baby were filled with the Holy Spirit because they were already overshadowed by the Holy Spirit.

Now, Mary spoke to Jesus and his disciples. Then Jesus, who had already received the Holy Spirit at this time, said, "It's not yet his time." Mary pushed him into his season.

Mary, the mother of Jesus, was full of the Holy Ghost; that's how she was able to preserve the gift she received from the Holy Ghost called Jesus.

Chapter Ten

Salvation for your Environment

Jesus Redeemed you from the curse, how about your Community?

Since the earth was cursed for the sake of man, was the creation also cursed because of man? This interconnectedness of all creation, bound by the curse, emphasizes our shared destiny and the need for collective redemption. God said to man, the day you shall eat of the fruit of the tree of the knowledge of good and evil, you shall surely die, (Genesis 2:17). When man ate this fruit, he did die, but not immediately. Man died spiritually, which was a separation from God, and eventually died physically, because the things around him, which were supposed to keep him alive forever, were denatured. When man died spiritually, to enable him die physically, his environment, and creation around him also lost life. We will discuss in detail, how creation around man started dying once Adam sinned.

One of the curses God placed on man before he sent him out of Eden was to till the ground. This means that the earth was automatically tilled on behalf of Adam before he fell. After his fall, the automatic nature of the creation, which was the God kind of life in them, a life that was in perfect harmony with God's will and purpose, was also stripped from them to enable Adam to die physically.

Since Adam chose death by eating the fruit of the tree of the knowledge of good and evil, creations around him that enabled his longevity, were cut off from the eternal life supply source, to produce physical death in Adam. To elaborate on this, when God created man, he commanded him to eat every seed-bearing plant and every tree whose fruit contains seed as food, and the animals and birds were also provided for, Genesis 1:29-30.

After man's fall, his diet changed from eating plants and trees to eating from the ground, including animals (Genesis 3:17). God changed the serpent's diet and that of man to facilitate the curse he laid upon Adam, which would eventually lead to his death.

The creation around Adam started dying first to facilitate Adam's death. The vegetation, the climate, the rocks, etc., which also had the life of God in them, had to be withdrawn into a different kind of life to enable Adam to die eventually. This is what apostle Paul was trying to say in Romans 8:20, "For the creation was subjected to frustration *and* futility, not willingly [because of some intentional fault on its part], but by the will of Him who subjected it, in hope". In other words, the creation around Adam had to be denatured, from their original state to the state of needing redemption.

Jesus came and redeemed man from the curse of Adam, now what happened to the creation around man? Were they also redeemed? Why did Paul say in Romans 8:19 that creation waits for the manifestation of the sons of God? The Greek word for sons is huios (hwee-os), which denotes legitimacy. It stresses the quality of the offspring, those who have Godlike abilities. The sons of God, as used here by Paul, are True or legitimate sons of God, those who depict the abilities of God. And those who exhibit that particular kind of quality that can only be found in God; his creative ability to help the creation.

In other words, creation is waiting for legitimate sons of God, those who possess his creative abilities to manifest. What are they waiting for to manifest? Creation is waiting for God's kind to redeem them from the curse. Jesus Christ redeemed man, but creation is waiting for man to, in turn, redeem creation from the curse. This emphasizes the profound responsibility and power that man holds in the process of redemption. It's a significant role, a consequential responsibility that we humans have. If not, man will continue to die around creation, which subsequently produces death because it is still in the cursed state.

If you continue in Romans 8:20-21, you will understand that creation was placed under a curse because of the sin of Adam and has long been under bondage until now; in expectation of redemption by the true sons of God.

What I am saying in essence is this: as a legitimate son of God, when you manifest your sonship, the things around you, the earth, the trees, and other living or non-living things around you, such as rocks, etc. will catch up the life of God in you.

You know, as a child of God, you exude or emanate the life of God (Zoe), a life that is abundant, eternal, and full of divine power. This life has the potential to transform and renew your environment, then your community, bringing redemption to your world.

We are all together, united by our shared destiny and the collective need for redemption. As Jesus Christ redeemed us, we also need to redeem our homes, communities, and the creations around us. While the world is crying for the help of climate control and change, creation is saying we know our redemption lies within the true sons of God, rise, and redeem your environment.

The Mystery of the Holy Spirit Upon your Mortal Body

Let me start by saying that what you are about to hear is a great mystery and mind-blowing. Jesus said to his disciples while teaching the people in parable. They asked afterward why he spoke to the people in a parable; he said to them, "For you, it is given to know the mysteries of the kingdom" Mathew 13:11. And no one will receive such mystery unless it is given to them to know it. Let us dive into the mystery of the Holy Spirit possessing your mortal body.

The book of Joel 2:28 reads, "And it shall come to pass afterward, that I will pour out my Spirit upon all flesh..." What happens after the Holy Spirit possesses your flesh is what happened to the disciples in the upper room.

Apostle Peter took it further by explaining to the people that even if you think we are drunk (you will act like a drunk when the Holy Ghost takes over your body), he said to them, we are not drunk; we are exhibiting what is written by the prophets in the book of Joel.

Apostle Peter explained to them that what they saw the disciples dramatize was what God promised to happen in the last days, which is happening now because it is the last days.

Apostle Peter states the day of Pentecost and what the disciples experienced in the upper room marked the beginning of the last days, a period of time in Christian eschatology that is believed to be the end of the current age and the ushering in of the Kingdom of God.

"But this is [the beginning of] what was spoken of through the prophet Joel: AND IT SHALL BE IN THE LAST DAYS,' says

God, 'THAT I WILL POUR OUT MY SPIRIT UPON ALL MANKIND; AND YOUR SONS AND YOUR DAUGHTERS SHALL PROPHESY, AND YOUR YOUNG MEN SHALL SEE VISIONS, AND YOUR OLD MEN SHALL DREAM DREAMS;" Acts 2:16-17.

According to Apostle Peter, the people watched them speak in different tongues and languages. They also prophesied, and he said it fulfilled the promise made by God through the prophet Joel.

But that's not what I am trying to tell you. The mystery is this: What happens to you when the Holy Spirit takes over your body or flesh? What do you think would happen to you when the Holy Spirit takes over your flesh and your physical body?

Consider what happened to Jesus of Nazareth. When the Holy Spirit takes over your flesh, the laws of the physical world cease to bind you. You are now under the influence of the Supernatural, and you will begin to perform acts that are beyond human capability. This is the transformative power of the Holy Spirit's presence on your flesh.

The Holy Spirit is an immortal Spirit, eternal and divine. His presence on your mortal body bestows upon you the gift of immortality. Your mortal body becomes immortal, a vessel for the eternal Spirit of God.

Look at it this way: Jesus, when he was raised from the dead, became immortal, could walk through walls, and was seen in different forms. The Bible declared in Mark 16:12. This means that the Supernatural, which is the manifestation of the Holy Spirit upon your mortal body to make it immortal, will also cause you to be experienced in different forms. Certain people will encounter you without knowing it is you.

Apostle Paul said it right when he said in Romans 8:11, "If the Spirit of him who raised Jesus from the dead dwells in you, he will also quicken your mortal bodies...." The Greek word used there as quicken is the word zoopoiesei; which is the combination of two words (Zoe = zoo + poieo) which is Zoe- life, poieo - to make. It then basically means this one thing; the Holy Spirit will make your flesh to become the life of God, a life that is characterized by divine power, wisdom, and love. Your flesh will demonstrate the true meaning of the life of God. It means whatever God can do; you can also do because your flesh has been revitalized. Your flesh has a different life, God's kind of life.

Now, you must go back and find out what the benefit of having this Zoe kind of life is, not only in you but also on you (your flesh). This can be seen in the major gifts of the Holy Spirit.

Your ability to manifest in the word of wisdom, word of knowledge, the ability for your flesh to heal other fleshes. Perform miracles, discern spirits, and have the ability to prophesy, speak in divers' tongues, and interpret those tongues (which also includes languages). All of these and more, are what would happen to you when the Holy Spirit takes over your flesh.

Chapter Eleven

Looking into the Future

The law of Salary Review (Jacob and Laban)

Based on his family's needs, Jacob got up and told his boss and his uncle that his family was growing. Though he didn't say it, he knew he wasn't getting enough money or pay to support his two wives and their kids. Jacob re-evaluated his job based on his family's needs. Even though he could have stayed with his father in-law and continued to manage and get lazy while his family suffered and managed one or two bedrooms, Joseph advised himself. He said to himself that as a royalty, his children needed to taste a different kind of life.

Looking into his children's future, Jacob, with the wisdom gained from his upbringing, realized that he needed to free his children's future from the bondage of servitude. His foresight and strategic thinking guided his decision to seek a better life for his children.

Reflecting on his own life, Jacob recognized that his ability to dream and aspire directly resulted from the opportunities his parents provided him. This realization emphasizes the profound influence of parental guidance in shaping one's destiny.

Jacob then advised himself, went straight to his boss, who was also his uncle, and said to him, we must move on now because my kids are growing, and I need to make room for them to learn what I learned from my parents, Genesis 30:25-30.

Jacob told his uncle Laban, "I must not live off of your own provisions as a man; I must also learn how to provide for my own family to avoid Joseph's mindset becoming distorted, Genesis 30:30.

Did you know that Laban provided for Jacob and his family until Joseph was born? In other words, his other sons grew up knowing servitude and slavery, and how can you justify that someone would continue to serve you and would not have any property of his own?

You know Laban, who was an idolater, said to Jacob that he learned by divination that God blessed him because of Jacob's presence in his household. But you would ask, why was he so dubious and reaped him off many times, though he knew he was the source of his blessing? You know he was a carrier of spiritual blessings from Abraham and Isaac, and even though he was serving, the blessing he was carrying still magnetized physical blessings towards him. In other words, Jacob's blessing was a spiritual blessing that physically attracted things to him.

Before I go further, let me tell you what happened here. Jacob knew that a special child would be born into his household, whom he must teach well because of his destiny. He knew he would have to teach certain things to him; if not, he would not have the wisdom to manage Egypt as a prime minister. He knew that for one to become a prime minister, he would have to learn basic skills as an entrepreneur; if not, he would not be able to manage a powerful country like Egypt.

Remember his mother had told him to go over to her brother's house called Laban and get a wife from there? His mother was a big visionary to Joseph's birth. Do you remember when she (Rebecca) had to ask the Lord about the troubles she faced with the babies in her womb? And she was told that there were two nations in her womb. Jacob's destiny was also revealed to her in this particular place, and that's why she had to work with him to ensure he attained God's purpose for his life. What I am saying in essence is, Rebecca was aware that Jacob was the one to carry the next generation forward. Esau would have aborted the next generation.

Learning How to see Visions and Dreams

When Rebecca noticed, through revelations, that Jacob was the next generation of Abraham, she knew she needed to protect not only Jacob's destiny, but also the destiny that would come from him; that's why she told him to go to her own brother and to marry one of his daughters.

In other words, the reason Rebecca told Jacob to marry one of her nieces was to protect the next generation.

Jacob knew when Joseph was born that he was a ruler and would not need to observe any form of lack or poverty; if not, he would grow up distorted because poverty or lack begins to distort children's minds from childhood.

Joseph's ability to dream of being in charge or being a leader would have been distorted if his father hadn't observed in time to make room for him to dream such dreams.

Jacob, being a spiritual person, realized immediately when Joseph was born that this child would rule even in a strange land as a prime minister; this was why he had to train him well. When others were busy pasturing, Jacob was busy with Joseph, teaching him how to be in charge and a leader. Jacob, who knew the power of vision and how to recreate things, began to teach Joseph how to be creative, beginning with his mind, then his vision.

You know, Jacob taught his animals to dream dreams, and they reproduce based on the power of their minds and what they focused on. His livestock multiplied based on the power of visions and dreams.

Look at what he did with Joseph. The Bible didn't say a lot of things about how he coached Joseph to become the prime minister of Egypt, but the Bible said he made a coat of many colors for him. This coat symbolized Joseph's special status and favor in his father's eyes and was also a spiritual tool used to initiate Joseph's mind in the realms of dreams and visions. As I said earlier, Jacob made his animals dream dreams, and he achieved this by building troughs around the location where they mate.

Jacob took trees and made spotted branches on them, and while the animals came to drink water, some would associate with others. While that was happening, they focused on those spotted tree branches, thereby producing offspring after their dreams and visions. This was supernatural help Jacob received from God when it was time to move on from his uncle, who was very dubious.

The power of the vision of the mind is not limited to certain species of animals, that's why you can train dogs to identify objects using their senses. This also tells you that when you sport or associate with your wife or husband, what you carry on your mind is what you end up reproducing. That's not the topic of discussion though.

I am trying to say this: in the same way Jacob made his uncle's livestock dream dreams and got his wage from them, he decided he would do the same with Joseph, whom he identified as a special child.

He made a coat of many colors for him, and immediately after he did that, the Bible says that Joseph started dreaming. This coat, to some, was a symbol of Joseph's special status and favor in his father's eyes, but Jacob understood the purpose. And the dream he was dreaming was the dream of becoming a leader, a ruler.

That's why when Joseph's brothers came and told Jacob the story that an animal killed Joseph, he couldn't recover from it. Do you know why? Jacob knew what God showed him about Joseph: that the survival of his generation would come from Joseph. So, Jacob was devastated because it meant he was at risk of losing the entire lineage.

That's why, when they requested to take Benjamin, he said no. He had begun to train Benjamin to see if he could dream like his brother Joseph.

As a point of reference, Joseph's big brothers, who were born and grew up under the servitude of Laban's house, were somehow influenced by that environment. That's why immediately after Joseph was born, Jacob said it was time to leave to prevent him from being influenced by the negative environment. Laban was also an idolater who had many wooden and carved gods and was a diviner.

Joseph continued to dream until his brothers took his coat of many colors from him. I just want to confirm to you that the reason he had those dreams was because of the clothing his father created for him. The coat of many colors influenced his thinking, which in turn caused him to meditate on superiority, and presented in the form of dreams at night.

As I was saying, immediately after this coat of many colors was taken away from him, he stopped dreaming. But because he had mastered the act of visions, he began to interpret dreams. This shows that the ability to dream is closely linked to the ability to interpret dreams. If you cannot dream in life, you can't interpret others' dreams. That's why it's dangerous to share your dreams with people who don't dream; they will kill it for you. That's what Joseph's brothers tried to do, kill his dreams by killing him.

What is Freely Given to You

Let's delve into this scripture from 1 Corinthians 2:12. It tells us, "Now we have not received the spirit of the world, but the Spirit who is from God, that we might understand the things freely given us by God." Have you truly grasped the depth of this message? In my understanding, it means that everything we receive is a gift from God. We cannot receive anything that has not been freely given to us by God.

Some of you see things, dream dreams, and wake up and throw them away. I want you to re-examine the things you throw away. God speaks through dreams and other channels. Be diligent about trying to interpret your dreams instead of throwing things away. You cannot receive it if it's not given to you freely as a child of God.

Also, you may see certain times in the scripture that the word would say, "and he opened their understanding" (Luke 24:45). If your understanding is not opened, you cannot freely receive anything. Pray that God will enlighten the eyes of understanding, so that you can understand what God is saying or has been telling you.

More so, you can know those around you, who do you more harm than good. What am I saying? I am saying that many people may be around you, but not all are for you. As God freely gives you something, the enemy is also moving freely to steal, kill, or destroy what God has freely given to you. As you dream good dreams and are blessed, the devil also freely steals from people through ugly and bad dreams.

In other words, when you dream, it's crucial to discern the source of your dreams. This discernment will guide you in knowing when to dismiss dreams and when to meditate and pray over them. Remember, not every dream comes from God. The devil also induces dreams to steal and manipulate the children of God. As 1 John 4:1 advices, 'Do not believe every spirit but test every spirit to know whether they are from God...'.

And I conclude by saying this: who or what is the source of your dreams? Who is the originator of the things you see and meditate upon? I asked this questions to get you to think, because even the devil can give you dreams. Oh yes! He did it to the woman in the garden. He was able to sell his dreams to the woman who started dreaming like him. The Bible said that the woman SAW that the tree was good for food, and pleasant to the eyes...Genesis 3:6. Her ability to see, was her ability to become or dream dreams.

What I am trying to say is this: whenever the devil gives you a dream, you have the power to interpret it. You can choose to see things from his perspective, which often leads to doubting God and disappointment. Remember, God had already created them in His image and gave them the name Adam (Genesis 1:26, 5:2), but in Genesis 3, they were given a different vision, and once they focused on it, the woman became it.

When you have nightmares and ugly dreams, it's just the devil trying to sell his visions to you. He wants you to imagine it and then start dreaming from him. But you were created with great abilities—to know and to choose. You can wake up from that nightmare or ugly dream and just take the word of God over that dream, speak it, and then it will cancel every satanic visions or dreams. The Bible is your guide, your reassurance in countering these negative dreams.

What do you think happened to Jesus in the wilderness? Satan gave him dreams and told him what to do, and that's why each time he said, it is written... it canceled whatever the devil said to him. In other words, you can't win the battles of life if you don't know what is written in the Bible concerning you. Open your Bible, find out what is written about you, and then conquer the world of negativity and fears. You can dream from a different place or source, but the Bible is your source of enlightenment and victory.

Chapter Twelve

Are You Rapturable?

Break the bondage of fear! You are a Child of God

The Revelation of Jesus Christ by John the Beloved outlines two crucial criteria for the rapture. The first pertains to those within the Church, while the second applies to those outside the Church. Let's explore the first category of people who are in the Church and will not be raptured. Remember, if you have given your life to Jesus and live the life in him, you are automatically rupturable. Whether you are struggling or not, it doesn't matter where you are in your Christian life; if you have the seed of Christ in you and do not fall into the category that I am going to discuss here, you are rupturable. This is a beautiful demonstration of the love and grace of our Lord, which comforts us in our journey.

Now, let's turn to the book of Revelation 2:19-25, and listen to what Jesus had to say to the Church in Thyatira, a city in Asia Minor. His message to them is not just a historical account, but a timeless one that resonates with today's Church.

Jesus started by acknowledging the works that this Church in Thyatira had done, the love, work, and services in the kingdom, but he said he had something against them. And this is the only Church among the seven churches in the Revelation that Jesus promised something regarding the rapture.

In Revelation 2:20, he said, "You have allowed that woman Jezebel, who calls herself a prophetess, to "teach, seduce my servants to commit sexual immorality, and to eat things sacrificed to an idol."

Jesus enumerated this offense as what people in the church have done. Their offense is that they allowed this woman called Jezebel (a spirit) into the church. In other words, this church knows who Jezebel is. Still, it has not only condoned her but has also allowed Jezebel(spirit) to practice seduction, which has led the servants of God into sexual immorality and idolatry.

Then, in Revelation 2:21, the Lord also said, "I gave her time to repent of her sexual immorality, and she did not repent," Meaning that an all-merciful God has also given this woman time for repentance. Her unrepentant heart would take her to the next Judgement, which is?

Let's look at the book of Revelation 2:22: "I will cast her into a sickbed, and those who commit adultery with her into the GREAT TRIBULATION, unless they repent of their deeds." This is a very loaded verse. First, we know by this scripture that it is the Lord who determines who will and who will not be raptured.

Second, we know that repentance is available for those who find themselves in this category. You can repent until that second when the rapture occurs, but since you don't know when it will happen, why don't you repent before it's too late?

Third, this adulterous woman called Jezebel will be in sickbed, including those who also committed adultery with her. And they all shall go through the great tribulation. This great tribulation literally means that the devil will be ruling the world. And you will not have mercy from the devil because there is no atom of mercy in him; he knows nothing like good or mercy, he is a very mean devil.

There is the word tribulation, which means persecution from the enemy; we experience this on and off as we live as believers in Jesus Christ. But the word "Great Tribulation" is totally different; it means the devil ruling over the world. It then means that the criteria as a child of God or a Christian to miss rapture is sexual immorality, adultery, witchcraft, and sorcery.

Also, in Revelation 2:24 the Lord said to this church, "...as many as do not have this doctrine, who have not known the depths of Satan, ...I will put on you no other burden."

Do you know what this means? It means, sexual immorality, adultery, witchcraft, and sorcery have become a doctrine in the church, and people have watered down the gospel of purity because of the teaching brought about by Jezebel, who calls herself a prophetess.

This scripture also says that those who have not known the depth of Satan will be spared from the great tribulation. Do you know what this truly means? That witchcraft has been in the church to the point that people practice witchcraft and satanism while parading to be children of God. It means you can no longer differentiate those who are deep in Satanism and those who are not because everyone professes to be part of the church.

You know what the Lord didn't say here? He didn't assign you to go after people digging to see who is satanic or who is not. He just said that he (the Lord Jesus Christ) will make them go through the great tribulation, where the devil, that old serpent, will rule over them.

To confirm that God has not assigned you the Job of digging into who is practicing satanism in the church or who is not, let's look at what the good Lord said in the book of Mathew 13:25 -28, where Jesus gave a parable which likened the kingdom of heaven to a man who sowed good seeds in his field, and while everyone was asleep, his enemy came and sowed weeds among the good seed. When they woke up (which is about now, the church was sleeping and now is waking up), the servants came to the good master saying, we saw you sow good seeds; who sowed the tares(weed)?

The master told them that the enemy did it. And the Servants requested from the master to authorize them to uproot the weed, but the master said no. Why? He told them that during harvest, you can easily differentiate between the good seed and the weeds. Because trying to uproot the weed now, you may mistakenly uproot both the good seed (wheat) and the weed together.

This is the typical example of what's happening in the church now, where you have murderers, thieves, and adulterers holding the microphone, or associated with people who are the servants of God. Even though you can pinpoint some of them, the Lord said, let them be, at harvest, we will know the good seeds from the bad ones.

In summary of this first category of people who will not be raptured, they are people in the church, who profess and deceive people that they are children of God, or Christians, but they are living in sin, sexual immorality, idolatry, witchcraft, which can lead you into the depth of satanism. Regardless of how you deceive yourself or others around you, Satan will have to rule over you when the church is gone. And the Lord is also saying that if you don't find yourself in this category, that burden of going through the great tribulation will be removed from you, but make sure you hold strongly unto what you have until he comes, Revelation 2:25.

As I told you earlier, the devil has no form of mercy in him because that nature does not exist in him. You know how you have a conscience and can see something as good, bad, or evil? The devil has no such thing in him called conscience, and that's why he can never repent.

He cannot turn around and say, "God have mercy," because he doesn't know anything like that. He only knows evil and wickedness; the same way many have known the depth of Satanism, they have known evil, and therefore, cannot repent either.

Do you know why? Their evil will not give them that chance to repent. That's why you can see some kill and continue to kill without remorse; it is because it's not in them to show mercy.

I will give you a glimpse of an example of what the devil can do to a person in one day, especially those who believe in God. Look at the book of Job 1, when God authorized the devil to the trial of his servant Job. One day, his sons were killed by the wind, and his wealth and assets were gone the same day before his actual trial started. (Job 1:8-20).

You see, the earth is still stable because God is still in charge; the devil wants to rule so bad that he can't wait to be given charge over the world. In the same way, many leaders get excited to rule over the nations of the earth; that's the same excitement the devil is foreseeing. The world will be handed to him to rule, he will be in charge for three and a half years. It will be a terrible experience for both those who believe in God, who did not get raptured because they were in a state of sin, and those who believed in the devil. He will also be destructive to those who believe in him, because there is no good in him.

As I said about Job, it took the devil nine months to reduce Job to a pauper. A man who was known for wealth and righteousness, was made a laughingstock in months.

You can also see what the devil is already doing to some people in families, how he can use some family members to destroy the whole family. That's what his abilities are now because he is not yet in charge; he only uses people and influences them with demons to carry out his activities on the earth. After the rapture, he will no longer need to use man; he will be in charge of his demons roaming all over the earth. You will see the physical devil and demon's manifest.

The second category of those who would not be raptured are those who have never believed and accepted Jesus Christ as their personal Lord and Savior. Yes, he died for them, but they just decided they didn't want anything to do with him. They were given multiple opportunities but didn't want anything to do with salvation.

Let's look again at the book of Revelation 9

These are the people who have witnessed all plagues upon the earth; they have seen many killed by insurgents, bandits, and armies from hell but still insisted on living the old past lives. They have witnessed the signs in the heavens and earth, seen all the atrocities performed on the earth as a warning for the rapture, but still ignored the signs.

The trumping of the seven angels and the plagues that followed afterward were all warnings to prepare people for the rapture. The prayers of the saints being offered on the altar before the throne of God in heaven, rising unto God, is a qualifying effect that the saints are crying unto God for rescue, for salvation. And the only way the saints can get these answers back is to prepare the earth for rapture.

First, the seven angels were released with the seven trumpets. Then, the earth was plagued so the inhabitants could repent and seek salvation. By doing this, many could be raptured. But part of the devil's plan is to prevent many from seeking salvation, blinding their eyes from seeing the need for salvation.

Apostle Paul discussed how the God of this world has blinded the minds of unbelievers (those who do not believe in Jesus Christ) 2 Corinthians 4:4. He blinded their minds to prevent them from seeing the light of the gospel of our Lord Jesus Christ, thereby preventing them from seeing the need for salvation.

In conclusion, regarding rapture, it is spelled out directly from the Mouth of Jesus, he was specific regarding those who he will allow to go through the great tribulation. But, since he is a merciful God, he has provided everyone with equal opportunity for redemption and the ability to be raptured. For the unbelieving, it is also their choice to repent and receive the gift of salvation, in the person of Jesus Christ.

Conclusion

Jesus Post Resurrected body

This book will not conclude without looking at Jesus after he resurrected from the dead. As our impeccable example, we focused on him throughout this book, and to conclude this book without looking at how Jesus concluded his ministry would be an injustice to this book.

You remember at the beginning of this book; we examined how Jesus' prayed for the glory he had from the beginning to be restored back to him, and for his disciples to manifest this same glory? Jesus concluded his ministry on earth by exemplifying to us what a renewed and glorified body is capable of doing.

In other words, to conclude this book, we must enumerate how God the father answered Jesus's prayers in John 17:1-26; and how he continues to answer those prayers today. Before his death, Jesus asked God the Father to restore him to his previous glorious state, which he called "the Glory that I had with you from the beginning" (John 17:5). God the father answered this prayer, and many more after his death.

Jesus was crucified, died, and was resurrected by God, but something unique happened post his resurrection; he returned with a new body. That glorious body he had with his father from the beginning, even before the world began, was what many couldn't recognize when Jesus was resurrected. The Bible called this "different form" (Mark 16:12), which is why they couldn't recognize him after his resurrection. He had to inform them and reintroduce himself to some of them to recognize him. At a point he had to break bread with the two disciples he met on their way to Emmaus, before their eyes were opened to the supernatural to recognize him, (Luke 24:30-31).

Now that Christ is risen, and you are risen with him, what form are you? What form do you find yourself in? "As he is, so are we in this world" (1 John 4:17).

When Jesus died, he was buried with grave clothes, meaning he was clothed like the dead. And when he defeated death, the grave clothes were also removed. Here is my question: Where did he get the clothes he was wearing when he resurrected? Was it his glorious body that was his covering? Was this the body that was stripped from Adam in the garden? If it is, it means that he also restored your glorious suit that was stripped off by sin in the garden when Adam sinned. Therefore, you are not naked, you are wearing a glorious body. The resurrected body is glorious, it walked through walls and did many things, and the walls should not limit you anymore.

Let us expand this information about Jesus Post resurrected body. After Jesus appeared to his disciple's post-resurrection, when they doubted whether it was him, he said to them, touch me; spirits have no flesh and bones. What Jesus was saying to his disciples here is that there is something that limits you as a man, which was imputed in you by the sinful nature, it's called blood.

Let's delve deeper; Lucifer, in the course of his trading and various merchanting, underwent a transformative process akin to a chemical reaction, the end product of which was sin. This sin, a profound transformation, is attributed to Lucifer, the originator. God encapsulated this transformative process in the tree known as "The Tree of the Knowledge of Good and Evil." The fruit of this tree, when consumed by Adam, initiated a similar transformative process, introducing blood to the human body.

In other words, Jesus' post-resurrected body was a bloodless physical body. Remember, he had already emptied his blood, which he presented to his father in heaven for the atonement of the sins of man. Do you remember the Book of Hebrew stating that this blood speaks better things than the blood of Able? (Hebrew 12: 24). Where is that blood speaking from? It's speaking from the throne of God. When you get into Mount Zion as enumerated in the Book of Hebrews 12:24, you will experience the blood of the sprinkling, which is constantly speaking.

I said all of that to tell you that part of the reason his disciples couldn't recognize him was because he was in a different form; he was a physical body that was void of blood. Jesus was clearly saying to his disciples here that blood limits you from manifesting this kind of life. Jesus the second Adam, who brought back what the first man lost to sin, was saying to his disciples that the glorious body, which can be limitless, was a bloodless body. The first Adam had only flesh and bones; that was all he needed to function on earth as God. Until sin entered him and corrupted that body, Adam functioned and represented God on earth. The sin of Adam was what introduced blood into the human body.

What am I saying here? Adam mentioned when the woman was handed to him, "This is now bone of my bones, and flesh of my flesh..." blood had nothing to do with the first man Adam until sin was found in him, Genesis 2:23.

Jesus, when he was trying to find out what his disciples knew about him, asked them a question, "Who do men say that I am?" and when they had answered him, he then asked them, "Who do you say I am?" When Peter answered him correctly, saying, "You are the Christ, the son of the living God." Jesus responded by saying, "Flesh and blood did not reveal this to you, but my Father in heaven" (Mathew 16:13-17)

Jesus here confirmed that blood has such a limit, and that it limits one's ability to truly manifest God on earth. Jesus 'statement meant one thing, that flesh and blood could not sustain and transmit the revelation that Peter received, it could only come from God, who is limitless.

In all of these information, I am saying that Jesus' resurrected body was bloodless, and that's why it was a different form that only the spiritual eyes could recognize. That body that worked through walls and translated into heaven was bloodless, and that's the same body Adam had before sin was introduced into him.

Why does Satan walk into your house without fear? He walks through your walls and is not even afraid, it's because he knows you don't know this part of you. Next time, when witches, the warlocks walk through your walls, they will meet something that will shock them to death.

The post-resurrected body of Jesus Christ is without limits, and the Bible says you are the body of Christ (1 Corinthians 12:27). Why then do you have limits? And who told you that you can't do this or that? Who told you that you are naked? (Genesis 3:11).

Apostle Paul said it better when he wrote, "We are members of his body, his flesh, and his bones..." Ephesians 5:30. Jesus has restored that body that you had from the beginning, the glorious body that could manifest the eternal life on earth.

Therefore, I say to you, like Apostle Paul, "Let this mind, which was in Christ, also be in you". You have been restored to produce eternal life, to give as many as you come across that eternal life (John 17:2).

Don't shy away from the purpose you exist for, stand your ground, you have been restored to replenish and multiply on the earth. You're not multiplying your own self; you are to multiply the Zoe life in you. You have risen with him and much more seated with him at the right hand of God the Father. Now do those things you couldn't do before and conquer the world for Jesus Christ. Rule in the midst of his enemies and make his enemies his footstool; that's why you exist on earth.

Shalom!

Printed in the United States
by Baker & Taylor Publisher Services